Russell Atkins

on the life and work of an american master

Russell Atkins

on the life and work of an american master

• • • • • • • • • • • • • • • • • •

KEVIN PRUFER & MICHAEL DUMANIS, EDITORS

ISBN 978-0-9641454-4-3

Published by Pleiades Press
Department of English & Philosophy
The University of Central Missouri
Warrensburg, Missouri 64093
&
Department of English
Winthrop University
Rock Hill, South Carolina 29733

Distributed by Small Press Distribution (SPD)

Cover Image of Russell Atkins © by Charles J. Pinkney
Originally printed on the cover of *The Chestnutt Record*
edited by Nathan T. Oliver.
Book design by Kevin Prufer

2 4 6 8 9 7 5 3 1
First Pleiades Press Printing, 2013

Financial Assistance for this project has been provided by the Missouri Arts Council, a state agency.

Contents

ESSAYS ON RUSSELL ATKINS

An Introduction

Just a little bit past Chester Avenue, right before Stokes Boulevard intersects with Euclid Avenue, is Fenway Manor. It had once been a grand building, rising thirteen red brick and sandstone stories over Case Western Reserve University on one side and the Cleveland Clinic on the other. Today it provides subsidized apartments for "senior and disabled living" run by a group called ABC Management. Across the street is an empty park: a cluster of trees, patchy grass, no benches. The wide streets around it are chaotic with traffic.

The sign below the red awning says "Private Property" in large, black letters and the door opens onto a white hallway, a couple soda machines, a closed business office, three restrooms, all locked up tight. To the right is another door and another room, this one suggesting something of the building's turn-of-the-century grandeur, a richly carpeted floor, a grand chandelier, little clusters of well-used furniture before each large, arched window. Sometimes, an old man dozed in one of the armchairs. More often, the room is empty.

On the eleventh floor of Fenway Manor, overlooking the Cleveland Children's Museum, is Russell Atkins' apartment. These days, he spends most of his time in an unadorned living room, where he's got a sofa, a twin bed of the kind designed for hospitals, a walker, a wheelchair in the corner and a flat screen TV that chatters on in the background. He hasn't many possessions on display—a few books, a couple black and white family photographs. The most treasured of his items he keeps in six or seven tattered cardboard boxes, some stacked in the closet, others placed at the foot of his bed.

Mr. Atkins is nearing ninety. He can't walk easily anymore and is sometimes attended to by a young, businesslike, very quiet nurse. He is thin and small, with a swirl of fluffy, uncombed gray hair. He has a slightly high-pitched, gentle voice, a voice that strains a bit to be heard. Visitors surprise him and he seems a little perplexed and astonished that several American poets think highly of his work. When he learned about the volume you are holding in your hands, he said, "Why, who would want to read about me?"

—

Russell Atkins was born in Cleveland, Ohio in 1926 and raised by his mother, his grandmother, and his Aunt Mae, whom he affectionately calls A'Mae, and whose portrait still sits on the table beside his bed. His father deserted the family and was, Atkins writes, "never seen by me." (In one conversations, Russell Atkins referred to him as "a maniac.") In a short autobiographical sketch, Atkins, who is African-American, describes his early days growing up on 76th Street: "a room kept with the shades down to protect my eyes when I was sick with diphtheria; a toy automobile which I pedaled violently up and down the sidewalk in front of our house." Atkins' aunt was a dressmaker and his mother earned a living doing housework for wealthy families in Cleveland, some of whom, Atkins recalls, gave him gifts of expensive clothing and toys.

Although his mother and aunt seem to have been dependable parents for the young boy, his grandmother, who thought of herself as a "light-skinned lady," was far less stable, increasingly becoming obsessed with the presence of a ghost (a "hant," she called it) bent upon darkening her complexion or, as Atkins describes it, "making her black." This hant, Atkins recalls, would also extend its malevolence to him, darkening his skin as well. "I remember her constant murmuring to herself all day (talking with the 'hant') and then, suddenly, leaping up and demanding that it leave the house and be quick about it! She turned race into such a ghost story of goblins and devils and religious quotations that it was impossible to take her seriously." This, Atkins says, reached a head when the delusional woman kidnapped him, the two of them hiding out in a set of dilapidated rented rooms until the police rescued him. "It was clear," Atkins recalls, "...that the 'little light-skinned lady' could not be trusted to take care of me." (Later, the old woman became obsessed with religion, and, after preaching and ranting in storefront churches, would disappear, Atkins says, for months.)

However, his mother and A'Mae seem to have created in Atkins a love of music and the arts. "They didn't necessarily encourage me to *write*," he told Kevin Prufer during one of their conversations in his apartment, "but they encouraged me to have a kind of freedom." He recalled that the household was full of music. His mother, who preferred classical, played the piano, and even bought a player-piano. Atkins remembers being fascinated by her sheet music, taking it out of the piano bench and spreading it on the floor, looking at the rows of little black dots. His A'Mae, like his mother a Southerner, was fond of blues, spirituals, gospel and would play those records on the phonograph. Meanwhile, Atkins picked out tunes on the piano or sought out jazz records, music his mother had no time for and distrusted, generally, as "naughty."

In 2007, Michael Dumanis moved to Cleveland to become the Director of the Cleveland State University Poetry Center, a literary press. There, he first encountered Atkins' work in the form of the collection *Here in The,* published in the Poetry Center's early years. The book was strikingly different in content and style from many of the Poetry Center's publications of the time, which tended toward narrative and first-person meditative lyric. Atkins' poems were formally experimental, elliptical in their phrasings, audibly influenced by jazz and in dialogue with a wide range of modernist and postmodern poets, alternately bringing to mind Marianne Moore, Langston Hughes, Charles Olson, Robert Creeley, Robert Hayden, Michael Harper, Frank O'Hara, and d. a. levy, though to be truthful he didn't really sound like anybody else. This was a poet interested in music and silence, favoring the fragmentary and disjunctive over the linear or finished, capturing distinctive diction and the mood of an instant.

At the time, there were fewer than twenty copies of Atkins' book left in the Poetry Center's offices (now, only archival copies remain). Michael thought it would be interesting to bring Atkins back to Cleveland State University's campus more than thirty years after the book's publication, but found out that Atkins was in poor health and not interested in making public appearances. He called him on the phone and arranged a meeting. At the time, Atkins was still living in a small, freestanding house at 6005 Grand Avenue, filled with shoeboxes and crates of manuscripts and correspondence. When Michael asked Russell if he had copies of all of his poems, Russell replied, “Yes. They’re all over this house. You’ll have to find them.”

———

The third time Kevin Prufer visited Russell Arkins—in 2012—he asked if he’d haul down a couple of his cardboard boxes.

“They’re very heavy,” he said as Kevin dragged one from the top of the stack and set it on the carpet in front of his couch. Then another. He wondered if they’d been opened since Russell had moved into Fenway Manor a few years before. Russell certainly couldn’t have budged them by himself.

“Here,” he said, “is a concerto,” paging through a brittle, handwritten stack of sheet music. And here was one of his many “Spyrytuals.” Then came the music that accompanies his verse-play *The Abortionist*, then another thick selection of his compositions for piano. Page after brittle page, hundreds of pages of intricate, neatly written music.

And then drafts of poems, poems folded into poems. “Could you put the poems in one pile and the music in another,” Mr. Atkins asked, and soon both piles were large, the first box nearly empty.

And from among the folded up drafts of poems fell a series of letters to Russell Atkins from Langston Hughes, perhaps a dozen written over many years, some quite lengthy. They were filled with news of Mr. Hughes’ travels to Florida and California, to Berlin and Yaddo. Sometimes Hughes asks after a poem or two. Other times he offers suggestions for possible publishers.

A little pile of neatly typed letters from Marianne Moore is next. These offer Atkins bits of advice (“Practical, somewhat inexpensive paper is the kind to use, I feel, rather than foppishly elegant keepsake rag and silk varieties") or criticism (of a draft of "Elegy on a Hurt Bird," she rather archly writes, "This shows what you can do. The motion and mood are secure—eloquent. Only the words detract.") Still other letters are more introspective. "One must not laugh at one's self, i.e. deprecate or ruin a hypothetical excellence by being tongue-in-cheek," she instructs him. "Few agree with me about this, clowning is the mode; but I am sure of what I feel—for myself. And I am in revolt against profanity and its false emphases … and I think I infer that you share my austerities."

A group of letters from Clarence Major are generally more succinct and direct. "You are," Major asserts, "one of the best poets I know."

"Do we have a stack for the letters?" Russell asks, and soon that stack is thick, too.

In the second box, there are more letters, more handwritten music. Old issues of *Free Lance*, of *Experiment*, of *Beloit Poetry Journal.* A photo of the poet as a smiling baby boy, another of his Aunt. One of a very pretty African-American woman; Mr. Atkins says with a smile, "Oh, her? She was a magician friend of mine." And nothing more.

After two hours, these two boxes are organized and Russell is tired. Sometimes, he can't quite hold onto the papers and they slide from the couch to the floor. Sometimes, he needs a little help getting the rubber bands around the stacks of letters. After a while, he asks if Kevin would repack the boxes and place them at the foot of his bed.

When Kevin rises to leave, there are still five or six unexplored boxes in the closet.

"I'm sorry I can't walk you to the door," Russell says.

——

As a young man, Russell Atkins had already benefited from not only his family's artistic interests, but those of several good teachers in the Cleveland public school system—teachers who took him to the art museum, who taught him something of the craft of puppetry ("I fell wildly into puppet making," Atkins writes), painting, composition. He memorized poems and took to reciting passages from Shelley, Bryant, Shakespeare—but never, he recalls, Byron. Byron was frowned on by teachers though, he told Kevin during one of their interviews, "I liked to imagine I *was* Byron." A moody child, he would often burst into tears for no clear reason, confounding his teachers and family. He writes of being stunned by the film *Snow White and the Seven Dwarfs*, of running around town seeing it over and over again, obsessively reciting from it, drawing pictures of it, going from classroom to classroom performing scenes for other children, "using all the voices," he writes. "I was Doc, Sneezy, Grumpy, and so on, including the Wicked Queen." He resolved to practice the arts, to study poetry and composition for the rest of his life.

But Atkins' high school years would prove tumultuous. He loved his music classes, loved the fact that the choir teacher was so powerful he could pull students out of other classes in order to practice their singing. He says, "In school, the teachers thought I had promise, that I was talented … whatever they meant by that."

Generally, however, Atkins refused to do required coursework and bridled at the restraints imposed upon him by many teachers. He was, he recalls, "a selfish child. A terrible person, at least by most people's opinions." At the same time, he was quickly moved by new, challenging poetry, having discovered Pound, Eliot, and Moore in Louis Untermeyer's seminal anthology *British and American Poetry*. He grew fascinated by the modern, dissonant composers, the avant-garde, Wagner, the works of surrealist photographers, Picasso's *Guernica* (which he saw at the Cleveland Museum of Art). Of his troubles at school, he writes, "I was never able to explain to people that *I* was in charge of myself and listened only to *me*. This caused me to be thought of as someone without gratitude for 'opportunities' which I had not had a chance to examine."

Even after high school, Atkins could not settle down. Unable to hold a job for long ("I could never again do anything like that! Hours away from my thoughts, art, self-fulfillment," he complained at the time), Atkins took courses at the Cleveland Institute of Music, hung about with other intellectuals, practiced his piano. "During this interim," he writes, "I couldn't quite decide on a focus for artistic practice ... Finally I concluded that I would emphasize sound in my poems and ... I would 'sketch' music to hold it in thought until I could notate it. Also, having become avant-garde (by others' definition), what was to prevent me from writing these poems as shapes? Thus, the dichotomy was put in my mind in which I would 'compose' like a painter and write poems like a composer."

—

Cleveland seemed a provincial, remote place for an up-and-coming avant-garde poet and composer, one who increasingly saw his poems published in highly regarded journals across the country. Although Russell Atkins rarely left the city, he felt increasingly isolated from the hotbeds of literary and musical creation, places like New York and Boston. He found salvation, though, in *Free Lance, a Magazine of Poetry and Prose*, which he launched in 1950 (modeled on the earlier avant-garde literary magazine *Experiment*) and co-edited with his longtime friend Adelaide Simon. Two decades later, *Free Lance*, still under his editorship, would be described by *Black World* magazine as "the only Black literary magazine of national importance in existence." Through *Free Lance*, Atkins corresponded with writers from across the country, including LeRoi Jones (the future Amiri Baraka), his early supporter Langston Hughes, and Conrad Kent Meyers, whose first work appeared in the magazine. And Atkins himself would publish much of his most challenging work in its pages, including his verse drama *The Abortionist* ("It cost us some subscriptions") and his ongoing meditations on *pyschovisualism*.

The publication of his essay on his theory of psychovisualism, Atkins would later assert, made *Free Lance* seem like "the ultimate in avant-garde incomprehensibility," though it attracted the curiosity and admiration of a number of musical types, among them Stefan Wolpe and Geoffrey Sharp, the editor of *Music Review*. Psychovisualism grew out a disagreement with his friend Hale Smith, a jazz arranger then studying musical composition at the Cleveland Institute of Music. Atkins would assert that musical composition was essentially *visual*, the mind comprehending music through image, creating image-based compositions to which sound was applied. Smith would assert the opposite, that composition was not an extension of visual thought. "Can serious composers honestly compose FOR such an organ as the ear?" Atkins would ask. Or, later, he'd write of so-called 'musical' composition: "We see comprehension machinery at work by which the tones attach themselves, although we fail to notice much of it because of the force of sound stimuli. Composing is a *deconstruction* method that is fixed for the 'mind's eye.'"

It was during this period, the 1950s and early 1960s, that Atkins began seeing himself as a poet whose work was filtered through his highly individual sense of the deep visual ground beneath what we call music, the idea that the word "music" is itself "basically meaningless." He would rarely leave Cleveland, but continued living with his various older female relatives, his Aunt Mae, his increasingly neurotic mother (he describes her obsessive cleanliness, her abruptly painting everything in the house white), his grandmother, who would be obsessed with her *hants* until she died. He still refused to take on a full-time job because that would get in the way of his need to create new things, to think and read and write music that might "get rid of melody—that lingering concept of a single line of tones." He worked briefly as an office manager at a small music school, but quit when the job appeared to become full-time, spending his hours in the Cleveland Public Library's Philosophy and Religion Division, reading voraciously, seeking out friends who could help him translate German texts that piqued his interest. He had to decline an offer to attend the Bread Loaf Writers Conference when he realized that what little money he had would have to go to his grandmother's funeral expenses.

Ultimately, Atkins' strange concrete poetry, his flights of audio-visual intensity, his idiosyncratic word-play would bring him some measurable success, a little withering criticism, and, generally, increasing obscurity. From the beginning, Langston Hughes, Clarence Major and Marianne Moore (among others) took real interest in his work and career, performing his poetry on the radio, teaching it now and then, offering, over many years, sound advice. *Western Review, Botteghe Oscure*, and other impressive literary magazines published his poems and verse dramas, though equally impressive book publishers seemed unattainable. And Atkins himself seems as amused by his rejections as he is pleased with his small acclaim. (When *Accent* magazine rejected his poem "Four of a Fall" with the complaint that its "restless, perpetual ingenuity acts to overwhelm rather than reveal," Atkins proclaimed, "My 'conspicuous technique' approach was working!") And as the era of the Beatniks and the Black Arts Movement helped to define the work of Atkins' contemporaries, Atkins himself, unwilling to bend to the style of the day—and seeming a little hostile to the Black Arts Movement's single-mindedness—fell increasingly by the wayside, ever more out of step. When asked about his relationship to it, he brings up the poet LeRoi Jones. He says he didn't resent the attention that Jones got for his work, but he took notice of it, and he recognized that his lack of interest in it undercut his ability to publish widely. "I was more interested in technique," he says. "People said 'racial problems are more important than technique,' but I couldn't agree. They were interested in conveying a message; I was not."

In one of the occasional reviews of his poetry, *Negro World* magazine noted in 1969 that Atkins' *Heretofore*

> … is an unusual book of poetry in that if Brother Atkins' picture were not on the cover, one would have a difficult time knowing he is a black poet. The evidence is not in the poetry—not in his use of the language; nor in his use of the so-called "vernacular" (the swearing, when it appears, is white intonated); nor in the rhythms he uses (the iambs and other footage metres range from Shakespearean to Eliotian with some Keats thrown in for good (?) measure…the two poems which are black-related, "Christophe," about the Haitian brother, and "Narrative," about John Brown, are both written as if by a Victorian era observer, and not a blkman dealing with his history as he should be about doing (blkartists are responsible to the blkcommunity).

A mere four years later, Leatrice W. Emeruwa would disagree in the pages of *Black World* magazine, complaining of Atkins' increasing obscurity, comparing his gift to Robert Hayden's, and asserting that we should not expect him to restrict his work to "racial rhetoric." "Clevelanders who remain in Cleveland," she suggested, "are usually omitted when it comes to national recognition in the arts" though she also noted that Atkins "has been to poetic, dramatic, and musical innovation and leadership what John Coltrane has been to jazz avant-gardism. His influence upon both Black and white artists has been tremendous for the past quarter century locally."

These assessments would, in some ways, echo advice Langston Hughes had given the poet in a letter twenty-five years earlier, when Atkins was in his early twenties: "It I were you, I would not worry about being a social poet. My feeling about poetry is that each poet should write as he chooses and not try to be something that he is not. Only if you think and feel socially should you try to write in that way."

In all, Russell Atkins would publish a handful of short poetry chapbooks, some from his own Free Lance Press, others from similarly small, often avant-garde leaning publishers, most notably Paul Bremen Books in London. His verse dramas (often accompanied by the directive "to be set to music") would appear in similarly small, saddle-stapled, "homemade" editions. His only "full-length" poetry collection, *Here in The*, would be published by the Cleveland State University Poetry Center and Cleveland State University would also offer him an honorary doctorate, citing Atkins as "an example to aspiring writers, a promoter of racial understanding through the arts, a lifelong Cleveland resident…."

He would go on living in his Aunt's house for sixty-two years in all, moving to Fenway Manor in 2010 when the house was seized and demolished to make room for Cleveland's growing industry.

——

One of the great pleasures of editing a book like this is discovering, along the way, that a writer we once considered obscure has, in fact, many ardent admirers who bring to his work a wealth of sensibilities and fine intelligence. Five of these have contributed essays directly to this book—Alden Lynn Nielsen, Tom Orange, Evie Shockley, Sean Singer, and Tyrone Williams. Many others offered support and encouragement in other ways.

Every year that Michael represented the Cleveland State University Poetry Center at conferences and book fairs, someone would walk up to him and ask, "Hey didn't you guys once publish that book by Russell Atkins?" Despite the book now being over thirty-five years old and completely out of print, it continues to attract critical attention. Poet and critic Joshua Ware, a lecturer at Case Western Reserve University in Cleveland, just this month enthusiastically reviewed *Here in The* for a literary blog, asserting:

> Atkins addresses the decay of a once great city and foretells the Rust Belt's continual decline as a result of the difficult economic effects of moving our country's manufacturing and industrial jobs overseas. Everywhere through *Here In The*, the poet surveys the city, its residents, and surroundings, noting how even traditionally beatific images, such as a sunset, can transform into something less gorgeous in the crumbling urban cityscapes.... [Atkins] creates a singular Cleveland-based beauty in his language and the sounds it produces.

To spur further interest in Russell's poetry, Michael began to give copies away to poets and editors he thought may be particularly interested in reviving the work. This is how *Here in The* first made it into Kevin's hands and how they began to contemplate a Russell Atkins volume for the

Unsung Masters Series. As news of this volume has spread, both editors have received quite a few notes to the effect that *finally* a book would appear that might bring more attention to this brilliant, idiosyncratic, highly original writer, musician, and thinker.

At the same time, it pains us to think that so much of Russell Atkins' material—hundreds of pages of handwritten musical compositions, drafts of poems, letters, photographs—are piled in dilapidated boxes and stacked in a closet in a subsidized apartment where even Mr. Atkins himself is unable to access them. (They are heavy and he is too frail to move them.) We feel privileged to have been allowed by Russell to examine his manuscripts in such detail, to share with readers some of his recollections and theories and concerns—and we are saddened by the realization that Russell Atkins now seems to have no family and only limited contacts with former friends who might see to his papers' preservation. It would trouble the world of the arts if the uncollected work of this already marginalized poet and musician were lost to future generations.

Kevin Prufer & Michael Dumanis
Houston, Texas & Bennington, Vermont
May 2013

The background material for this Introductions comes primarily from Russell Atkins' entry in *Contemporary Authors Autobiography Series*, the contents of his boxes, Joshua Ware's appreciation of Atkins on the blog vouchedbooks.com (dated May 6, 2013), and Kevin Prufer's interviews and conversations with him during 2012-2013.

A Folio of Poems

Russell Atkins

Looking into one of Russell Atkins' boxes of music, poems, letters, and ephemera, 2013

ABSTRACTIVE

                    I came upon that gate
that tracery'd gently into open

there lay the sum of the dearest
once belonging, the memoried
that scattered, then, compilingly
length',d into the poor pale

no place to bring one's birth
this hill they let run down
among them where the scant
droops to astray with dearth'd

                    the one and one,
a four, or ten even and seldom'd
wisp'd across listened into grass

there where   only
                    as a grey amount
coming on with swerve
solemns afar   whole family
again
            my dear ones

from *Here in The* (1976)

AIR DISASTER

                    under
more of sky
appearanced
a crack   quick'd
then roses of horror
whole dimension's plumb
swift flecks air

alarm plumes up   stark'd
against   all boards
abuzz   fainting
of wives with children
mothers'   mothers

there in a thunder
a too thick of aghasts of dust
over the field—
ambulances, fire's fire!!!
roundabout clang
and a siren flamingly
eeeeeeeeeeeee s

from *Here in The* (1976)

ANGLES

they are patient   and hold grudges
somewhere far down old transit lines,
or crossings, where an oncoming diesel
dangerouses; involuntary looking streets,
mum of a dark window   framework

the all directions of afraid
                —compasses, measuring tape,
one angle in particular
from the head and shoulder
then feet-first straight
a few inches, openly small

—the time at which lines make a point

having closed in a matter
of minutes

from *Here in The* (1976)

CHANGING SEASON

Arrives as if to drive a hard bargain
around the first of November—
that in a plain dark suit   the hair
greying in a flurry   he fends off
complaints with cold authority,
willing to listen—but, he says,
the contracts have been drawn
            —opens his briefcase,
hands out statistics to reporters
—things look bad,
like stocks falling, banks crashing,
            he'll meet with all:
"I know," he says, "but that's
the way things are—"
                                he is angered,
his body tightens up in a breezy
overcoat   he has other appointments
and much ground to cover:
a conveyance pulls up (a woman,
with vermilion hair, sits
in the back seat)

there's no getting around it:
he has the last word

from *Whichever* (1978)

ELEGY TO A HURT BIRD THAT DIED
[Buried in a Matchbox]

I suppose you suppose that yon of little burial
Is non of? Rather it is of universal o'er
Unvast because it unvast looks?
Well, how wrong, sir. How it propounds
Means utter, confounds, evers,
Wee-rosed as it is, alas,

I suppose you suppose, as some,
It was one of the lone
Who did thus? Ah yes,
As if one's boned
Sleletal'd in uneager sands
On shores undroned.

But we are other of
"Little Bords," each undone:
Laid in his "matchbox"
At last, at last no one.
Why if living bird dies
Should I not solemn him?

Bird, you shall be wept
For too. I do. From dogs,
Children, the cat, we made
Hurried away. Fragiled
In hand—I knew then—
Too frail a bloom.

from *Objects 2* (1963)

EVENING REFLECTIONS IN A BIRDBATH

still   there in our birdbath
strangely eye-like   light
repeated from the sky
ill of it there is the   so small
touch of a world's beware

some leafy shadow overs
from trees wind swell'd,
the yard commonplaces
now
        household sentiments,
              a rake, the lawnmower

until more stark than ever
in the round of the bowl
the always terror
stares out
        and out
with a *lo!*

from *Here in The* (1976)

FLU

1

An expeditionary encampment
                                                where men huddled about
a pillow of the snow's precipitous ascent.
                                                They lit a fire:
they shared the whiskey that burnt cold
                                                 —arms hands busy
keeping found twigs ablaze, flashlights
                    that startled out with the rectangular.
There was a squall to be —
                                                shudder of lungs
sensed that it may come down with whir
                                                swarming the bedclothes.

2

all was near hush
about the room:
this *was*, I'm sure—
moreover,
they stored
the gold—
source of monetary systems:
                                                they wove
                                                the probabilities
                                                for all time
                                                every computer
                                                spinning
the uranium
was kept there
                                                the heavy
                                                hydrogen
nerve gas

3

much in the sound of coughing
upbroken of pieces, not organization—
in a sudden of a laugh to a cough
a whizz'd of ski, flying snow filaments
the back hotels   fear them
                    there, men age to coughs,
shifting alone in drears of beds
and in their soiled underwear:
a kind of truth about themselves hacking
(no self-sacrificing wives about)

but summer parties, bright houses
coughs may be deliberate there,
                                        social—
accidental too—drink which slips
from the gullet
                                        show-like
gargled fears down a path
                                        unknown to me:
in the by-ways of the throat
                                        a mugging

from *Whichever* (1978)

FLU AS AN OLD WAR MOVIE

They're *the* strategists! They first clamp
Off the food supply from the port:
Heavy gunfire around the gut warehouse,
Like guards stabbed, one whipped cold
                                        with a gun butt.

They seize the camouflaged brain radio
Scrambling the signals. Anyway, signals
Can't get through.   With flame throwers
They close in and in and tight.

While brain waves burn, a crack
Lung Team hits at breath.   They reconnoiter
Spraying the lobar regions—cold gook
From their Chemico-Warfare Division!

They've got one objective: the big
Muscle Center whose dynamos—
    huge pericardium masses—thunder
                                        until whack,
    light is zapped, electricity's
    out—
            something it out!

from *Here in The* (1976)

FOR A NEIGHBOR STRICKEN SUDDENLY

There are murmured about his lawn
—the lawn he kept meticulously chiseled—
impossible scratchings and voices once,
suddenly, the *only* possible ones
as the shards and paper wads,
        the filtered leaves, those who pass
        frowning in recall of him

Measure his blood pressure then by
                        the wildest tendrils
            both overgrown
                     both by the cruel'd edges

The house, like damage in his brain,
commensurately stricken—
            there, too, like a memory trace
            is his forgettable lawn

from *Here in The* (1976)

FOUR OF A FALL

1

A lavatory. I waited.
A dare of a mirror quivered with light.
(They're waiting for me, I thought,
the old ones at the hearths.)
I said hesitating, 'Ten o'clock, Ed.'
I stood and thought of conditions
and of a conversation with Ethel
(Ethel was Ed's girl friend).
I had said to her, 'This business, life,
terribly exaggerated—'
                                        a low sigh
from about. I went and I
tried the door. (—my whisper,
'What in th' !! are you doin'?'
'a (shit—'
'—hurry it up, will you?'

He remained silently in. I was weary.
He came out very long after.
Our eyes thundred together—his, 'junk' full.
He was extinguished in a way,
but gave me a succession of brilliant replies.
We departed as the toilets pounded.

2

One night of a mass of harsh sky
I went with him through deaths, wine, sex.
A 'profound' tree let Last's beauty
funereally fall. It was autumn.
There it was, dead dark, of full slut.
Night houses poured their prowl.
He leaned to err. 'You are tendrils,'
I remember I said to him, 'dead near a wall.'

That night I stopped him and I said 'Listen
a moment—let me tell you:
you will never live it. Alas!
It is a Niagara of falls
to men that persist, headlong over.
Turn an ear like warriors who hear
the trumpet of a truce.
Come upon the suddenly sheer.
The merciless incessant underneath,
forth from it a persuasive horn
bays to the desperate.
Then who can help?'

3

One day visiting him as we effected a trip
to some authoritative cure, I said to him
in at the door, 'Hurry, will you?'
Agitated, the outstretch of his arm.
His face an unassembled horror
on the bed. 'But lemme tell ya, I ain't sick!'
'We want an authoritative cure,' I said.
His limp over a chair. 'I'm straight!'
he cried. And disgorged bilious black.

He was one night grim statued at my door.
He came to sell. One in the grey
who took the lamps down, lay in wait,
spider'd across, adder'd among.
It turned to storm, a mad tear up.
An ominous of rain shuddered from a banged sky.
A flight of lightnings
Swift'd terribly across.

Within I said, 'I never will inflict upon myself
that punishment you bear.'
He said it made bright dawns in dark of a winter,
smoothed the harsh, cleared the blear.
Did I—(he faltered)—want to—?
No! I told him. He fierced up.
I said, 'So you would tomb up me!'

4

A rush of miserabled leaves!
Some gasp, terrific fingered trees
skeleton'd after and left that white Medusa
stone hideous above, ringed in her mist adders.
The expanse of the eternally buried we passed slow.

This night he had peddled his asps
and we were walking among murdered leaves.
He paused. I said, 'What are you waiting for?'
He said, 'Show me about Ethel.'
'Who would want you addicted? You've lost her!'
He became violently utter
and he droned, 'Be Ethel to me.'

A moment violently stark
it fled—with it
                        I

Dated October, 1953
reprinted from *Heretofore* (1968)

IDYLL

snow brings restraint
and takes you by the arm:
snow's religious, morals over
the landscape, relaxes
with a minister's smile
and its hands folded
across a great belly

unlike authority
elsewhere, snow will
not keep a pair
of handcuffs

snow hates the body
and fashion

from *Here in The* (1976)

IMAGINARY CRIMES IN A REAL GARDEN

a spring already short of breath
on its way to asthma'd summer:
                                        I gather
allergic grass and shrubs' roots
sterile from last year (no rainfall'll)
help them, no hope from water)
                                        useless beseech by boughs:
a blueberry bush asking, pleading;
faggots in a bunch, their necks,
snap of twigs' necks   crunched
                                        thick earth—
between the hands, against knuckles
(a fat man's squeezed trachea)
a bough woman's fetus,
a shape of a female twig
                                        break her
slow, painful   scream of rape
a feminine squirming
                                        I shove
them down   bind the bag

with a short wire
                                        this is the kill

from *Whichever* (1978)

IT'S HERE IN THE

Here in the newspaper—wreck of the East Bound.
A photograph bound to bring on cardiac asthenia.
There is a blur that mists the pages:
On one side's a gloom of dreadful harsh,
Then breaks flash lights up sheer.
There is much huge about. I suppose
        those no 's are people
      between that suffering of—
      (what have we more? for Christ's sake!
Something of a full stop of it
crash of blood and the still shock
          of stark sticks and an immense swift gloss
And two dead no 's lie aghast still
One casts a crazed eye and the other's
    closed dull
            the heap twists up
    hardening the unhard, unhardening
    the hardened

from *Here in The* (1976)

LAKEFRONT, CLEVELAND

The stretch cast out night's long,'d
a hideous voyage of far
under'd sepulchral sky,
colossal as a grave's after. I
stood by a monument of thrust rocks
shouldered together, that tremendously
vaulted and rent themselves over sea

There was extremed
wake of the city
(a woman
                    somewhere having secreted her burden
        cast in her toilet
a jellied foetus—
        a surgeon's blade
hysterically sharp)

waves slid away
a murmur of laps
        —there lo! saw I
it—pulp

There, as stretch cast out night's long,'d
and hideous voyage of far
under sepulchral sky
collossal as a grave's after,
this pulp came down
that wake of city—

Now, then, God, listen: I'd swear
I heard, heard low,
its sigh-sounds lapse
as from furious determination—

furious, horrid determination!
Though stretch cast out night's long;
though hideous voyaged afar;
though there was extremed
wake of the city;
though there's excruciation
under sepulchral sky;
though there is grave's after
and grave's before, I heard
I swear, some of furious determination—

heard go the sigh
before I swept it to muck
with a laugh of cry!

dated 1954
reprinted from *Heretofore* (1968)

LAKEFRONT, CLEVELAND

so thunders sea

it gathers strength
summoned   ascends   huged up
                    then *softs*!
curls up about rocks
upcurls about thick
about bold   curls up
about it
then dangerous'd soft!

sea gathers strength
summoned ASCENDS UPHUGED
               over whatever's round
CRASHES ! ! ! !
curls up about rock
upcurls about
at bold abruptly
curls about it
               softs!
dangerous 'd
               so 'oft
               too soft almost
summoned   ASCENDS UPHUGED
CRASHES ! ! ! !
curls up about rock
               softs
furious'd but soft
          too soft   *whist*
almost
          WHOOM! whamming everywhere
it gathers strength
summoned ascends   huged up

SPLASH about of bold
upcurls about rock
rocks about impetuous'd ! !
curls
curls up about
softs
dangerously
too soft with a
shudder

from *Here in The* (1976)

LATE BUS

Theft's hour—the bus
against the hark lights
afright from houses!
Two dark men board laughing
(their teeth, crooked)
and take a seat in back,
two men in jeans, jackets:

the streets are deserted:
the bus blunders on, bounced!
                    —we wait:
the men sit   still:
One talks to the other
yeah, —their eyes (—sure,
we know what's up—)
one feigns awhiled of sleep,
one coughs quickly as a signal
while the other holds—
now!
—watch their pockets,
their hands are moving:
one as for a cigarette
and one as if finding
matches
          he reaches, reaches up
falsely to pull the bell
cord   East 55
they leave the bus

it makes no difference:
four dark men board
                    —laughing

from *Whichever* (1978)

LOCUSTS, CRICKETS THIS SUMMER

someplace in a disaster of grass
a minefield made audible

                    a singular clicking
miniatured in the backyard
like the tick a minute before
                whole of its night
                        as a time bomb
or rifle lock
                    a booby-trap

from *Here in The* (1976)

THE LOST SCARF

A cursing thunder of gloom came across from
  then an hysteria of rain after.
Up from below, a shuddering gigantic surge!
The stark wrapped up whole of an evening of the fall.
I wore a dirtied, restless'd scarf (sentiment, though,
  loved it).
Wind reaching out of that garden of forever—
  that half of hollow'd of the fall—
  got it and shredded it, spectred it through
  the hideous blur; agonized it on the dead,
  rustled lawn, tortured it against, convolved it with!
It then disappeared by the tomb of the Rhones!
It had hung among souvenirs, lately been of occasions
  (the memories of which I was fond).
I sought it, the loved, over, about, beside
  soft, treaded the coffins

from *Here in The* (1976)

NEW STOREFRONT

Afresh'd with paint, the shop had glare:
chrome-plated the squared of for sale,
angles, or with glamorous rounds.
                                        Auto Supply Co.
The owner looked too outright
(dart of a much refracted stare).
Aluminum had set him blind awhile—
the false going virtue of hope

no public interest anywhere about

his innocence   among the smokeshops
the parlors of the barbeque, the bars
and barbershops proliferous.   All these
dives without sheen and more secret,
sinfully wised, merely glimmered

he dared their margins with silver

from *Here in The* (1976)

NIGHT AND A DISTANT CHURCH

Forward abrupt
                              up
then mmm
                        mmm
wind mmm m
         mmm
                      m
upon
the mm
                  mm
wind mmm m
          mmm
into the mm wind
rain now and again
the mm
                  wind
         ells
b
             ells
         b

dated 1950
reprinted from *Heretofore* (1968)

NIGHT AND A DISTANT CHURCH

Forward abrupt   up
then mmm mm
wind mmm m
        mmm   m
upon
the mm mmm
wind mmm m
         mmm
into the mm wind
rain now and again
the mm wind
bells
       bells

from *Here in The* (1976)

NOTHING DEPENDABLE

The changes of the year had been many:
there'd been no snow—not yet.
"Do you suppose," I spoke to a neighbor
"there's going to be snow?"

She said, "It's winter isn't it?"

But I was not convinced. Calling
"Will there be much snow—you
newspaper weathermen know everything?"
They said, "No probability tonight."
(Was that exactly what I meant?)
"Isn't it late?" I said, "seasonally?"

They hung up.
Sure they were hiding something.

the mailman who brought news:
I laughed but nervously,
"Still no snow?"

"It can stay that way.

And he was gone, gone without an inkling.
In spite of all, I sensed,
ominously, that it was a critical year,
that snow was in a trap
somewhere between now
and Armageddon
but no one
absolutely no one
knew

from *Here in The* (1976)

NOW SWEET CATHY

Now sweet Cathy
Is pouring beer here in a bar
Pouring beer in a bar
Where hard workers are.
Endure costs her; her dreams fewer,
Cathy with promoted bust is mature.

Cathy, ceased now
In yielding of honey,
Is dedicated to her
Baby and steady money.

Cathy, I shall cruel.
You will old, you will woe.
And beer obnoxious grows,
Hard workers drear.
Cathy, Cathy! (she's too mature to hear)
Could I but whisper in her ear:

Reality's Is, is but Is alone.
We confect it a body
For the bones!

from *Objects* (1961)

ON MY PHOTO

hasn't a chance   as if the face
turns on him and with crimes
that he did not commit—unless
there are the two of them?
—one who'd rob the local drugstore,
strangle the widow who has the money

the way the rascal loves the camera,
the garbled side of his features,
then makes a break
                    he's damned clever!
takes to the lens, then beats the rap

the innocent and modest one
now faces a judgment for the other

that's the way isn't it,
that one shall take the blame?

from *Here in The* (1976)

ON SEEING CYNTHIA AGAIN

Ah, Cynthia it is! ("Was" I should say.
"Was" it is.) Cynthia, Cynthia!
How have you been? (How she has, alas,
Is seen. "Has-been" I should say.)
Still beautiful? Still beautiful.
(Let me describe her. Think of a horse.
That's Cynthia. Horse? No, worse.)
Cynthia, I have thought of you, and I
Have thought of what could have become of you.
(What has become of her? I would say
Nothing has. Nothing, of course,
Becomes her.) Remember, Cynthia,
Remember the times of old?
(She cannot place "of old.") I know,
Cynthia, yes, you look as young as young can be!
A baby?! You lucky, lucky, lucky—
(Having a baby's (the most to say)
Commonplace as day). I certainly shall
Have to come and see it.
Where do you stay? (Well wherever,
May she be kept there and off
The thoroughfare.) Cynthia, you look
As you did once by St. Vincent's brook.
You have not changed at all.
How is matrimony? Of course.
Milk and honey.

Cynthia, it has been exquisite seeing you.
Give my few friends my love
(That is if I can send enough.)
Goodbye. Don't let the baby
Catch anything and die.

from *Objects* (1961)

OUT OF JOINT

not with his wife at eased
on the refresh of his front porch?
        not painting about
the house? not tying up the dog
with a wave of respectability?
not watering his lawn?

but out here with
pieces of red aglow, leer, on
the creased pavements, boozed over:
        sleazys of nightclubs
and not of our neighborly path

        he furtives by
unnoticing   urged to a prowl,
gargoyled with desires:
        his companion
unseeming   as a relative
unseeming   even as of old friends
        or of a family
that visits after church

        they furtive beyond
talking of "bitches"
talking of "ass"

from *Whichever* (1978)

OUT OF PATIENCE AT THE OUT-PATIENT CLINIC

the lively soiled dishes
pile the food carts with obstacle,
the bedpans under in a clamor

the paraphernalia for oxygen rolls
with grim
a patient looks bemoan

it is now four o'clock p m
and from the sheen of surgery
sweep the wonders of medicine
aloud of voices
"SEE YOU AT NINE—"
"SEE YOU TOMORROW, STEVE—"
"I'LL LET YOU KNOW—OH—BILL—"
(from debt, aloof: buying a farm near Oregon
or going to the Bahamas for the summer)

ha haaa aaaaaaaaa
afar in an office
there's a laugh

from *Here in The* (1976)

PROBABILITY AND BIRDS

The probability in the yard:
The rodent keeps the cat close by;
The cat would sharp at the bird;
The bird would waft to the water —
If he does he has but his times before.
Whichever one he is he's surely marked

The cat is variable
The rodent becomes the death of the bird
Which we love
                    dogs are random

from *Here in The* (1976)

REHABILITATION BLDG. ENTRANCE: FOUR O'CLOCK

I was, say, bound
for anywhere   anywhere at all
committed to more of above, above
the worse, when many of them,
sick against broken, broken-up
as from crash or a fate
of birth, with paralytically
askew limbs   came:
to sight drastic'd a lo and behold:
where were both should be legs?
nor for grasp his hands or hers
of these, and one grisly'd,
as in a kind of plastercasted
skin, came no to all living looks!

so bound
for anywhere   anywhere
committed to more above the worse,
how, to one's view, sudden mishap
crooked! Cruel'd sharp! Ax'd
as of monstrous'd vex.

then they were the miserabled gone:
the many of them   sick
against broken, with things
thus being   being
loudly unspoken

from *Here in The* (1976)

SCHOOL DEMOLITION

shot through
the windows
—murdered?

so silently
about the rooms
the autopsy
    begins —
the moon coroner
working
      late

from *Here in The* (1976)

SHIPWRECK

With today's sympathetics who can be
dare?
in the old days when sailed struck,
sank, who knew?   few, comparatively
(—no speaking cabinets,
much less "typographical" compassion)
But these days terroring,
the grim fashion's that the speaking cabinet
and the typographical
leave what sympathetics more than fear?
—dawn sheds appear'
on broken, strewn, muted in oil and algae
sarcastic'd to a shore—ducks death,
fish death; the senses even
aver the air's dark-ages' legions;
—sheep,
too, strange away, dying:
midnight trains farewell of track
stealth back with deadly loads;
—woe-ing
its worst all yesterday,
a multitudinous famine!

(as for long life and as for love?
list with the undertaker, thrumming
numb, undering through the hush
—what is more shipsunk wept for?)

be dare, sympathize—
even if it is
unwise?

from *Here in The* (1976)

THERE SHE SITS

There she sits the long day
Opening books, shifting (alas)
A thousand old pages
(and quotes incessantly).
Look, so spectacled—
        she's dull-eyed,
        sickly—!

"But what in God's name's the matter?

Ah Whitman, she's the alack
Of Muses. Tried to be
English even.

"Oscar and I, you know
We wore our differences?

Listen, she is quoting!
"Let us go you and I—"
She does but little else.
All's beneath her.

"For heaven's sake! O Muse!
It pains me. Her's once
The ear into which I
Said everything hugely.
She was fearless!

No more. We must whisper.
She has professor's ears.
Not so loud Walt, will you?
Walt! Wait!

"Listen, dear Muse, to me!
I'm Walt Whitman!

(she smiles
merely)

from *Objects* (1961)

TRAINYARD AT NIGHT

TH UN DER   TH UN DER
the huge bold blasts black
hiss insists upon hissing insists
on insisting on hissing hiss
hiss s sss ss sss sss ssss s
ss sssss ssss
when whoosh!
the sharp scrap making its fourth lap
with a lot of rattletrap
and slap rap and crap—
I listen in time to hear coming on
the great Limited
it rolls scrolls of fold of fold
like one traditionally old
coldly, meanwhile hiss hiss
hiss insists upon hissing insists
on insisting on hissing hiss
hiss s ss ss sss sss s
sss s s
s

dated 1953
reprinted from *Heretofore* (1968)

TRAINYARD AT NIGHT

THandUNandDER TH and UN and DER
      TH   UN   UN
      andDER   DER
its huge big bold blasts black
hiss insists upon hissing insists
on insisting on hissing hiss
hiss s sss ss sss sss ssss S
ss sssss ssss
when wh OO sh
the sharp scrap making his fourth lap
with a lot of rattletrap
and slap rap and crap—
I listen in time to hear coming on
the great Limited
it rolls scrolls of fold of fold
like one traditionally old
(coldly meanwhile hiss hiss
hiss insists upon hissing insists
on insisting on hissing hiss
hiss s ss ss sss sss s
ss s s
s

from *Objects* (1961)

TRAINYARD BY NIGHT

A THUNDER
then huge bold blasts bluff
hiss, insists, upon hissing insists
on insisting on hissing hiss
hiss s ss ss sss ss ssss s
ss ssss sss
when whoosh!
the sharp scrap making a fourth lap
with a lot of rattletrap
and slap rap

I listen in time to hear coming on
the great Limited
it rolls scrolls fold in fold
like the traditionally old

hiss meanwhile hiss
insists upon hissing hiss
on insisting on hissing hiss
hiss s ss ss sss s
sss   s s
s

from *Objects 2* (1963)

WHILE WAITING IN LINE AT THE BANK

Qualified for the officer's glaring,
His unsteady mind on his revolver.
(That's responsibility's difference)
Brute hysteria quite likely.
                                        From the teller
It goes waveringly, of a flutter
—farewell money!
It's in the streets and City Halls
Anxious places with all the fears

Now there's a circuitous break:
Systems analysts are working at it.
They needn't be as responsible
Nor as officious in the schema.
It's a natural enough probability:
That which gives money takes it away.

Dark importances have risen:
No safety, there's no stopping all this.

Now, money's as hard as rock
                              —is being done
Everything that can be done
To save the continent,   the earth
                    —water comes metamorphosizing
All's changed to a tenuousness
Pitched against quasars

"Teaspoonfuls weigh tons."

from *Here in The* (1976)

WEEKEND MURDER

sex pants are what she wears:
each night she tightens them on,
leaves with a flaunt   sexpants
have to be taken by surprise,
they are so uncannily aware

when she's asleep, they're up
convulsing with energy   I've
stealth'd but to behold them
out at night when closets
have long hushed to shut
—despicable twists
lewd'd across hangers

wasn't long, and I had them,
these sexpants, under a shower
                        for wet sexpants
are powerless
                                sun up'd
she asked, "Where are my pants?
Yes, the blue ones?"

                (had they but drowned!
not on your life!) and she,
she dried them to a starch,
tightened them on and forth'd
left with a flaunt (sex pants
not only have to be surprised,
they must be slain)

late, suspensed of the hour,
I seized the beast's buttocks—
for it's here that sex pants
spin, convolve, and madden and bedevil!
and did they scream in fear
ghastlying the bilged air,
opprobrious shrilling
slithering a chair's arms,
or flustering, thitherd—

I compelled them down
and with a blunt oblong
bashed   I bashed them
        to a squish!

from *Here in The* (1976)

YOU ARE ENTHUSIASM UNTIL THEN: DISCO

Quiver, shake out neckties and hair
with energy and rumor passing—
do not hold back, be as awkward as it is cold:
with heat, dress for the dirty-minded.
When you have taken to pauses,
to a maturity's identifications,
naturally, that shall be the stroke
for stern disapprovals, for inner sentencings
in still places while you wait
for the lone of judgment's voice!

Until then   you are enthusiasm
                              the dream
for the uncommitted ones who watch you,
compromise you into their perceptions

Quiver, perturb with forces anything
uniform and with whores and others' wives
deliberately handle yourself for fucking,
the billows of the vibes spill over you
the stimulus of gin and Scotch whisky.
You are where the booze is and while dancing
insist upon baring your ass!

to make the sense you have to, go and lose!
(—adolescents, the young adults
forcing all devils up a tree)

until the inner sentencings,
stern disapprovals awaiting the voice
of lonely judgments—

you are enthusiasm   until then

from *Whichever* (1978)

WORLD'D TOO MUCH (IRRITABLE SONG)

Bus hollows on   of back windows
awidth'd where oxygen, gust'd,
crosswise of neglect, a joyous'd
foregone of seats, the while a beer can's
joust'd about the floor's rubbish'd
and a driver's on the last run
as of fatal'd alone—
            how such cheerfuls me!
then someone boards
            there's always somebody

                        Once, woods'd,
(hazed by a dell's emerald'd,
that is, pastel's from a green rain)
aloned hush had banished heard,
no one for hours! Perfect, I thought,
such Garbo! —until
I saw someone afar'd, somebody by
—again

Cloister of a library's mum,
the half mute books rigid'd
with what's ceased, held;
and worlds-away of noise was thrill
as shunned   when eh!
another entered   sat
(—and wouldn't you know—)
somebody *always*

                    Even in dreamt
yons from a shores'd escape,
silent'd in a noon's sequin'd shining
in a rowboat's bask

(out on what enormous'd
for a thirst beyondful of sky)
— until
a motorboat's distanced appear
—always—always

So, to go to
Tibet's chill aloft
within a cave's chapel'd
high in the lull from earth'd
(as vale) for such Garbo! Safe?
useless:
There'd be a somebody
a Tibetan
—by-and-by

from the papers of the author
(with the following handwritten annotation: "*genus irritabile vatum*")

Manifesto

Russell Atkins

1) The practise of an art should be immersed in the bringing-into-existence-as-creativity process. The *result* need *not* communicate.

2) Art should be conditional, i.e., conditions set by the artist. Once set he should not risk these conditions for what is called "communication."

3) Art should encourage mannerism.

4) Do *not* encourage "economy" in poetry.

5) Rhythm in poetry need not be "smooth" or "musical" (since that word has a questionable meaning). Be cautious of these descriptions as a so-called "good ear."

6) Do not allow "precision" of observation and literalness as "sense" (i.e. exegetical reasoning or "good" logic) to interfere with or dominate experimentation or expressiveness, i.e. do not destroy a poem trying to make it clear.

7) All voice qualities should be acceptable as the poet intends them (ironic innocence, bombast, intelligence, etc.) However, do NOT accept understatement, "plain-spoken," prose-like as being "sincerity."

8) Be self-indulgent as an artist. Use solipsism if necessary—be the source of everything.

9) Repetition: Use *redundancy*. If a thing is good enough to be said once, it is good enough to be repeated in some form immediately and thereafter. What a reader "already knows" or has "already been told once" should not be a criterion for a poem's processes since a poem need not be determined by, or directed toward, "meaning" or so-called "sense" either as "economy" or as information. The poet may, like the composer with a melody, tell his audience the same thing as many times as he chooses using different words (like different orchestral instruments), or the same words in the service of rhythm, momentum, mood, *stimuli extension,* written volume, etc. Make use of "implicitness" since a poem is not obligated to avoid inherent meaning similarities as though they have already been written into the poem's words. Most grass may be "green" but the word "green" has its own properties.

10) Distract the reader. Generally, the casual reader goes straight for the "sense," or the "meaning" behind the words (as some alcoholics want to get full). Thus words as *performance* should intervene with "bouquet" or any kind of "conspicuous technique" with "meaning" secondary.

11) In Poetry-Drama (not "poetic" drama) the aim is similar: *the predominance of the poetry performance as technique!* Do not use "measured prose" (to quote a well-known critic) thereby leaving the poetry as an appendage of some play which would be self-sufficient without the poetry or measured prose).

Therefore:

12) If possible, avoid saying anything in poetry as it would ordinarily be said (unless as dialogue in the nature of quotation, or for contrasting effects). In short, avoid the language "really used by men" in everyday affairs ("the language of ordinary men," etc.) that's not far from the "grossness of domestick use" (therefore breeding contempt from familiarity). Question also "the language of common speech," to quote others. Rather, let poetry thrust toward a language "peculiar to itself."

13) ART: Art does *not* have to *convince*. Its aim is largely AESTHETIC, not essentially informative or "problem solving," or trying to "tell anyone anything." THEREFORE: "beauty," being its own value, is to be defined ONLY by the artist as he immerses himself in the bringing-into-existence-as-creativity process. Nothing the artist does is obligated to "work" for or "communicate" with an audience. It is a phenomenalism about which the audience is *relatively* free.

14) Art: Each artist—as creator—says: "This is *aesthetic* as I see it!" Do not confuse subject matter with Art: they are two separate entities. The art aspects should not be confused with "sincerity": the two things need not be the aim of each other in spite of all the nonsense about this. Art may be the treatment of subject matter and as such evolves intangibly through the artist as he brings-into-existence-as-creativity

that from the sublime to the obscene. Art may be logically in the nature of ornament as in many cultures. There is no reason for poetry to avoid the nature of ornament.

15) Don't write the "good" or the "best" of anything. Write poetry or "music" that does what YOU want done.

from *Juxtapositions* (1991)

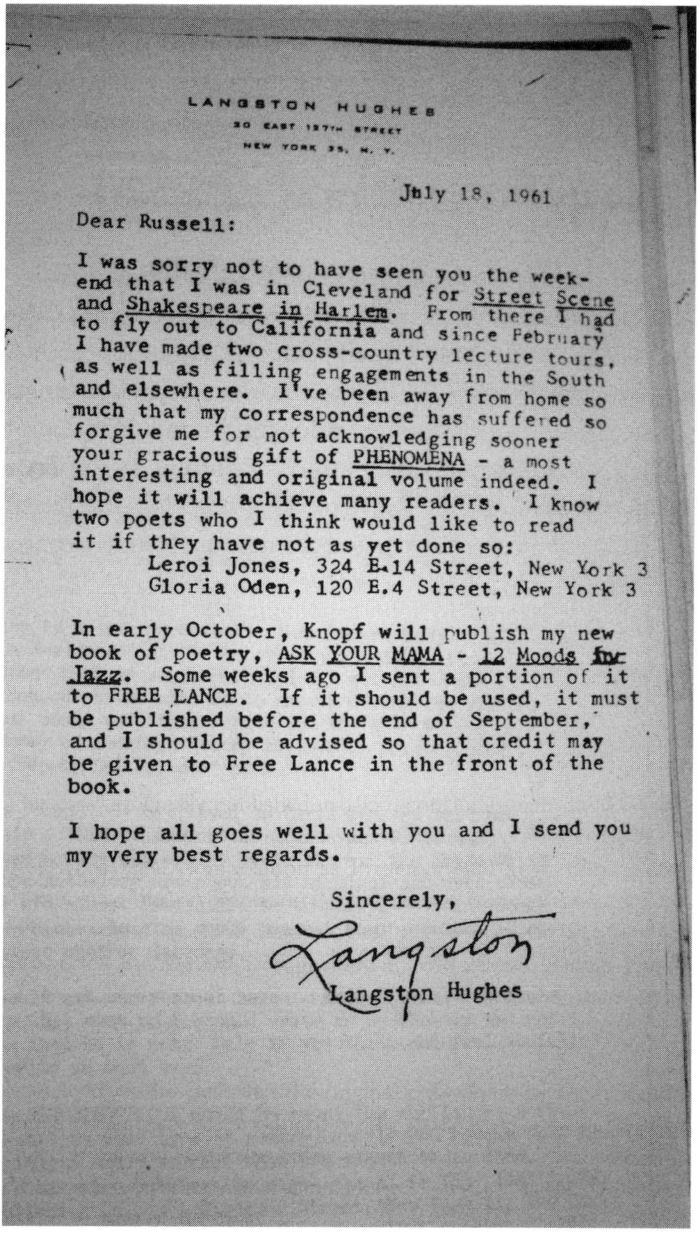

LANGSTON HUGHES
20 EAST 127TH STREET
NEW YORK 35, N. Y.

July 18, 1961

Dear Russell:

I was sorry not to have seen you the week-end that I was in Cleveland for Street Scene and Shakespeare in Harlem. From there I had to fly out to California and since February I have made two cross-country lecture tours, as well as filling engagements in the South and elsewhere. I've been away from home so much that my correspondence has suffered so forgive me for not acknowledging sooner your gracious gift of PHENOMENA - a most interesting and original volume indeed. I hope it will achieve many readers. I know two poets who I think would like to read it if they have not as yet done so:

Leroi Jones, 324 E.14 Street, New York 3
Gloria Oden, 120 E.4 Street, New York 3

In early October, Knopf will publish my new book of poetry, ASK YOUR MAMA - 12 Moods for Jazz. Some weeks ago I sent a portion of it to FREE LANCE. If it should be used, it must be published before the end of September, and I should be advised so that credit may be given to Free Lance in the front of the book.

I hope all goes well with you and I send you my very best regards.

Sincerely,

Langston

Langston Hughes

Russell Atkins' copy of the music for *The Abortionist*

The Abortionist

A Poetic Drama to be Set to Music

Russell Atkins

Scene: A basement in a half-deserted building in a deteriorated, dark, old section of downtown in a large city.

DR. DRASSAKAR (on phone)
Dr. Drassakar. Well. Miss Harrington. You're late.
I'm all ready. Near here you say? Then watch.
There are the down steps. Then the door.
Recall the bell? When you arrive ring it.
Don't neglect the bell. It tells me it is you.
Good. Come quickly, Miss Harrington.
(he hangs up)
Were she Dr. Harrington himself
Other first-staged beforehand would rear me to
the occasion!
(he then addresses small mice in a cage, sticking small pieces of cheese into the cage)
At last we take the lamps from Harrington!

(Drassakar next applies himself to the preparation for the visit of his patient. He rolls a battered operating table behind apparatus in a corner of the room under a light. This position obscures the table all but the head. He draws out of bag various instruments. He does this and more with a rather wild air about him. He is contemplating a hypodermic needle when there comes a ringing of a little bell. He grows ruthlessly active. Unlocks the door, then hurriedly seats himself behind desk. There is a knock.)
Come in, Miss Harrington.

(Enter Cecilia Harrington, face hidden somewhat behind coat collar. Young. Nervous.)

DR. DRASSAKAR
Sit down, Miss Harrington
And why do you tremble?
Let me help you—your coat—
(rises to assist)

MISS HARRINGTON
No, no. I won't take long, Dr., for I—
That is—I—well—I
Have something to tell.
It's of—we understand,
My decision?—you see—
That is—I mean—

DR. DRASSAKAR
This is but nerves, I say.
For now, relax, Miss Harrington.
The instrument' s temporarily off-key' d.
Talk of something—
Grow calm and—

MISS HARRINGTON
Hear me. Dr.! Our plan's a fang through me.

DR. DRASSAKAR
Ah now, Miss Harrington, listen:
Don't let the commonplace
Distress you. Remember,
These days strain you,
I say then look to a beyond
Of cheer. Vision the unspoiled,
The beautiful, the rose-of.
You have listened to talk.
Listen, however, to a man
Who knows, who has, as a
Master of it, of ruins
Lifted again; to disgrace
Given mask; to no more
Afforded more; to discords
The resolutions found.

MISS HARRINGTON
Dr., of course. You only
Meant to help. I know
For I came to you at will.
I am thinking of a father.
It will be a Lisbon horror
To him; the Vesuvius
To crush his at heart
For me! To tell mother
I'm to have a child,
To tell her that, for all,
I have no husband—
That he was without—
Without honor, will
Make stone of her.

How shall I say—?

DR. DRASSAKAR
Miss Harrington no fear
Of that, have no fear.
Just don't say of course!
You have attended my counsel?
Hush will be hooded
Over it. Only you and I
Will know that Cecilia Harrington
Was to have a child.

MISS HARRINGTON
This you don't know—my decision—
I will have the child
Dr.,—

DR. DRASSAKAR
Will have it?

MISS HARRINGTON
I have passed Highland Glades-Upon-Wieck
It sat stoned up in that Blank.
I commiserated passing.
Was I not responsible
More than to myself? Should I
Respond to the occur?
I have always wanted a child, Dr.
It waited to love, I thought. I
smoothed my hand on it.
In a grim sudden, Dr.
A death was more-of.

DR. DRASSAKAR
Miss Harrington, such sentiments

Oppress me. You, you and
Beautiful; the gem of a
Generation and a father
Famous throughout, surely,
You think how propitious
The universe is—All is, Ha!
Miss Harrington, don't be hasty.
Nine shadows of a year
And this texture of yours
Vanishes (he rises abruptly)
Bruted about, dilated
Swined in the sty—

MISS HARRINGTON
Dr., I— I—

DR. DRASSAKAR
You don't want that, Miss Harrington.

MISS HARRINGTON
You must listen—

DR. DRASSAKAR
You can't mean else.
(places himself against door)

MISS HARRINGTON
You don't understand. I forbid—

DR. DRASSAKAR
You forbid it do you!

MISS HARRINGTON
Do you ask for money?
Here tonight? You've assorted, readied,

Undertaken. Oh, forgive me!
Thoughts have built up a
Pillar of me. This terrible thing!
I won't think more of it.

DR. DRASSAKAR
Did I mention money?

MISS HARRINGTON
Are you detaining me, Dr.?

DR. DRASSAKAR
Hoping to exact a debt I
Thought of you. You will pay?

MISS HARRINGTON
Tell me the cost.

DR. DRASSAKAR
In money, Cecilia Harrington?
In pain!
(locks door. She reaches for it)
What's to be said for you?
Be calm. Do not resist
(he seizes her)

MISS HARRINGTON
Dr.—!

DR. DRASSAKAR
Sit down!

MISS HARRINGTON
You're a madman!

DR. DRASSAKAR
So you would slander the Dr.?
(he forces her into a chair; he lifts a glass from the table containing a liquid)
Miss Harrington, drink this, will you?
(forces her to drink)
This will incapacitate you,
Of course.
(pause)
(Cecilia Harrington, her head held in her hands)
Consider your self my patient,
Will you? What of patients? I
Remember some recovered;
Paid the bill; conversed with others similar. Dogs!
What a low of conditions!
I hated them.
(Cecilia Harrington, head yet in hands)
Miss Harrington, can you hear me?
I'm scorpion'd for revenge.
So you shall feel it sharp
Violating the sanctum.
(Dr. Drassakar bears her to the table across the room. There he proceeds in a violent manner to tear off her clothes)
Lie beautifully corpsed, will you?
That is assume the cadaver of him.
Ten years in debt, Miss Harrington!
The interest's just short of
Death. Let me tell of the debt of your father.
Yearly it changes a season in me!

Ten years ago, Dr. Harrington grew famous.
What on? Ideas thieved of me,
From a confidence of ours.
I was famous awhile.

Your father, Miss Harrington,
And I, once together
Engaged in questionable
Business—this business!
To extinguish me, he, Dr.
Harrington, your father,
Occasion'd it all over
But that on me the sinister contours looked better.
I professionally died.

MISS HARRINGTON (delirious)
Here's something—something very
mysterious—think more of it—
I've always wanted a child—
infinitely possible—

DR. DRASSAKAR
The drear'd heath of an ever of birth and success!
To one the womb. A gross, Miss Harrington,
A gross of years!
(there is violent action at the table: she screams)
So weed it out!

MISS HARRINGTON
Help me!
(she screams loud and long: he comes out downstage, his hand bloody, holding the fetus)

DR. DRASSAKAR
Miss Harrington, it is all over!
(he places the fetus in a washbowl. Cecilia Harrington moans in delirium)
This will kill him—DEAR Harrington!
(starts over. A rap on the door. Dead silence. Cecilia Harrington moaning deliriously. The rap is repeated)

NIGHT WATCHMAN
Dr. Drassakar!
(silence)
Xavier the night watchman, Dr. Is everything alright?

DR. DRASSAKAR
What do you want, Xavier?

NIGHT WATCHMAN
Making the round Dr., I thought—

DR. DRASSAKAR
Excellent. Everything is proper, I hope?

NIGHT WATCHMAN
Yes, well, that is— I—
(Cecilia Harrington thrashes on table. Gives short cry)
What's happening in there, Dr.?
(Drassakar hurries over to Cecilia Harrington. attempts to stifle her. Struggle. The sound of things falling. She gasps. Short screams. Drassakar strikes her to floor. Knocking on door insistent)
Dr. Drassakar! Dr. Drassakar!
(She is writhing on floor. Bust and head visible)
Dr. Drassakar!
(night watchman pounds the door. The pounding stops. Dr. Drassakar listens toward door. Cecilia Harrington moans. Drassakar turns. His eyes catch sight of the fetus. He proceeds to lift Cecilia Harrington up from the floor behind the table. Seizing the sheet from the table he wraps it around her shroud-like. She is faintly protesting—places her in armchair on full stage. Blood colors the winding sheet)

DR. DRASSAKAR
You are a mother, Miss Harrington.
(clothes fetus in a cloth, thrusts it at her)
What when the newspapers tell the story!?
Sit up here, girl! Falling about won't help.
Madonna of the Chair! Look up! Ugh!
You're impossible!
Here is the child. It's too bad
Harrington can't see you. I laugh at you!
Harrington will hate it!
(sound of footsteps)
They promise the police, Madonna of the Chair!
(there is a hurried sound of about five men. Their voices are confused. Drassakar stark)

NIGHT WATCHMAN
In here!
(terrific pounding)
(Cecilia Harrington slumps dead in the chair. Fetus falls to floor)

VOICE I
Open up in there!
(terrific pounding)

DR. DRASSAKAR
You can't save her!
(Drassakar hurries to Cecilia Harrington. Examines her)

NIGHT WATCHMAN
I have brought the law, Dr. Drassakar!

VOICE II
Let's break it in!
(there is a crash against the door)

NIGHT WATCHMAN
Again!

DR. DRASSAKAR
(leaning over Cecilia Harrington)
Dead
(curtain begins to close slowly)
(the door weakens. Drassakar retreats. Picks up knife. Door falls open. They face each other. They advance. Suddenly Drassakar rushes upon them. There is a shot. Drassakar falls among them as they bear him to the floor.)

The Abortionist was originally published by *Free Lance*, a magazine of poetry and prose, in the Spring 1954 issue.

A Psychovisual Perspective for 'Musical' Composition

Russell Atkins

Psychovisualism does not try to frame new concepts. It is chiefly preoccupied with adjustments: adjustments that might make a composer several times surer of effectuality. The following is a condensation of the general tenets of a psychovisual attitude toward composing and sound.

Of all people, the artist might advantageously increase his knowledge of the creating 'mind.' It is more obvious today than ever that the power of 'music's' impressive communication lies outside of the very element that transmits it, sound, and has far less to do with objectivity in the combinations of that medium than presumed seemingly behind 'musical' practices. Though it is said to be common knowledge (and there is little doubt that it is) the psychovisualist wishes to reaffirm that the creative process is not apart from its constituents, and might appear in this perspective's hypothesis as the very nature of a paradox wholly responsible for the pleasure received of 'music'.

Psychovisualism, while not new in detail, occasionally, in its total perspective comprises a radical departure from the ordinary academic view of 'Music.'

In the interests of American 'music' it might even be said that Europe, being the parent of much 'musical' pedagogy, based that phenomenon on terms that represented what, during the limitations of a time, seemed to take place. That many of these terms have a basis will be shown. However, that basis is not the one ordinarily thought of.

That American music schools must persist, or prefer to persist, in a semantical figuration derivative of European beliefs, contributes to the dependent nature of American 'music.' The question of cultural intermingling, being as it is too large for this limited discussion, I must assume that an American 'music' has ambitions of its own. To a psychovisualist it appears sometimes that European methods, for all their accomplishment, have not been thoroughly enough cross-examined in regard to American spiritual vitality. This is not to deny more or less esoteric investigations in musical matters by eminent scholars both European and American. It means that as far as the general 'musical education' is concerned, there has been little practical action toward lessening the influence of tradition as it practices its underhanded insistency.

ERROR OF 'MUSIC'

The psychovisualist find it increasingly difficult to accept the term 'music' as actually representative of other than improvisation or 'written for the ear.' He prefers to investigate the conditions existing between three things which he feels have become confused in rank: sound, music, composition.

The psychovisualist concludes that 'music,' contrary to

its presumptions as 'organized sound,' is the antithesis of composition. There is, to a psychovisualist, no appreciable validity in the term 'musical composition.'

The origin of the term 'music' scarcely seems to justify its position as that of intentionally organized sound on the part of a composer. By the term 'mousike' the Greeks signified many things compositely. None of them, however, qualify as mature Composition-and-Sound. 'Mousike' was more or less a scientific matter related rather to sounds as found in nature (today's frequencies, partials, etc.). A 'musical composition' to a psychovisualist is one that is based on a science of sound. Such a 'composition' makes use of relationships imposed out of a pure world of noises, tones, et al. Such a 'composition' can be constructed on a distortion of such relationships which becomes, in its way, an opposite aspect of the same science of sound. Such a world has no significantly expressive form-meaning. It is a collection of raw materials. The composition must be made. In short, the psychovisualist contends that the small meanings that may be made to exist in an absolute world of tone relationships are derived from a larger more significant phenomenal world: Composition As Object-Form. (Schism in modern music is that it will not conform to the old relationships of tonic pulls, scientifically demonstrable, and yet refuses to give up objective order of sounds as 'Composition.') The psychovisualist recognizes therefore that 'mousike' among the Greeks was meaningless relationship in sound and the derivative term 'music' plus 'musician' is used by him to describe a user of tone relationships objectified by nature, primitively arranged in a discursion that is called 'ordered sound' without significant form-meaning that comes only of a larger more significant world: Object-Forms. This is, only secondarily, a universe of sounds, but primarily a universe of objects.

The term 'music' persists, however, as a definition of

things it does not define, creating a figurative error that has guided the 'music' world for centuries. It has forced into concept the notion that sounds can be ordered by, tone system techniques. To this end there has been a great deal of 'composing' of 'music' with sounds. Liturgy, chanting, etc., forms of speech-song, did not improve matters. As the psychological possibilities of Composing began to appear the medium of sound demanded that 'composing WITH sounds' develop a syntax of a kind to attain higher order. Assumption that there may have been a greater relationship between language and sound-order than between the latter and anything else, finally expanded itself into monodic harmony with many presumptions, some scientifically demonstrable, concerning sound as organized. Harmonic syntax was no sooner established than psychovisual implications started to threaten the making of 'music' WITH sounds. In its place, clearly visible for the first time, what had been obscure: that Composition and sound applied was quite radically different from 'music.' Then and there 'music' as presided over by Muses, as tone-system, as a 'language,' received a deathblow. To the psychovisualist 'Music' is passé. He purposes a day of absolute Composition

COMPOSITION AND SOUND APPLIED

To a psychovisualist, the only intentionally organized sound on the part of a composer is Composition, which is not a binaural art but a VISUAL ART. In short, so-called 'musical composition' is a VISUAL ART.

How then is it seen and where? The more complex explanation of psychovisuality revolves around how and where Composition is seen.

Say, for example, two intensities, noises or tones, are heard. What meaningful relationship exists between them?

The ear distinguishes, relates their partials. Of the rate of vibration, a differentiation called 'pitch' is established. It could be supposed easily that this 'pitch' solves the matter, for there is, then, certainly a 'high' and a 'low' of degrees that suggests a relationship. The greater frequency of vibration the 'higher' the tone. The smaller the frequency the 'lower' the tone. The adjectives ' greater' and 'smaller could be replaced. The 'faster' the frequency of vibration the 'higher' the tone. The slower the frequency the 'lower' the tone. The words here that concern the psychovisualist are the words 'higher' and 'lower' and where they enter. Tones cannot be found existing actually in an objectively dimensional space of related positions. A 'high' or 'low' tone has existence among frequencies. There is only vibratory rate.

The psychovisual composer accepts that 'high and low' is imposed by psychic phenomena on tones as a primary condition for meaningfulness.

To the psychovisualist here is the validity of Composition as distinct from 'music'; for music, fundamentally, is the wrong assertion that meaningful relationships for Composition exist in sounds independently. Proof of their invalidity as compositional materials is, of course, the music of modern composers. 'Fundamentals' to tonic diatonicism, and that as tonal relationship only too suddenly upon the heels of a tempered 'pitch' compromise, proved, if anything, to be merely 'music,' not composition, and has been discarded in all but one way; a distortion of these relationships has built a world of sound emphasis which has become, in its way, merely an opposite aspect of the same kind of science of objective sound-order.

By these things it may be understood that the psychovisualist believes that much that is taught as 'music' is simply a naive study of that truly important phenomenon, spatial relationships for conception.

Another bane of 'music' to the psychovisualist is that without exception it is written FOR THE EAR. THE PSYCHOVISUALIST CANNOT TAKE SERIOUSLY ANYTHING WRITTEN *FOR* THE EAR.

In the light of the foregoing belief in the psyche as the apparatus for form, and form conditioned by space relationships and those relationships depending upon both objective and introspective visuality, it suggests itself that the ear cannot appreciate ARTISTRY.

The ear, a mechanical organ responding to vibratory rates, differentiates between intensities. It can differentiate between many intensities. However, the psychovisualist is not altogether certain that the ear is responsible for differentiation of pitch as 'high' or 'low.' The ear is not a conceiving organ. It knows nothing of depth or height, organization, or geometrical relationships visually. It merely differentiates between intensities and fast rates and slow rates of frequency. Musical practice, however, has not been anxious to dissociate pitch from 'high' and 'low.'

Can serious composers honestly compose FOR such an organ as the ear?

It is a major tragedy to psychovisualists that many modern notators do so (and that many composers of the past did so) and thereby are not (and were not) creating Compositions, but writing 'music.' Mere harmonies or tone-system techniques are construed as Compositions. These are described erroneously as the 'tools' of the 'craft' and even become construed as automatically Expressive of Something if the harmonic technique is elaborate enough to delude the writer that he is composing. That he expresses he never doubts. This, of course, derives from dividing the constituents of the creative process in reverse. Composers today find tone-system techniques or 'tools,' construe these as Compositions and sit back waiting for them to express. The process is actually the reverse. The Composer wishes to express something. The thing to be expressed suggests a mode of composition. A mode of composition evolves harmonic technique. It is assumed that a composer does not compose unless he has something specific to do or say in each Composition. However, he understands that having 'something to do' is not evolving tone-system technique as a thing important in itself.

There is very little else in Composition but Composition and to be a 'musician,' contrary to belief, is no advantage. One composes for sound as for paint, or stone. The false assumption is that composing and sound applied is different: that is of a phenomenon independent of visual conditions.

For all its accomplishments, the composing-and-sound art has supported and is even yet supporting what seems to the psychovisualist, a few misinterpretations of its functions, the primary fallacy being that there is an art for the ear made with sounds.

That sound-art is a visual art to the composer, and a composer, one who compose for sound to be applied, is psychovisual visual in perspective.

Now that we have suggested Composition as opposed to 'music' we might better investigate Composition itself.

If all tones vibrated with the same frequency rate, say, slow, little differentiation of composing value would exist. Fast frequency rates supply slow frequency rates with points for reference. Slow frequency rates are slow because there are rates that are faster. If it were not so, slow frequency rates might not be termed 'slow' or 'low.' However, once understood as 'slower-than,' differentiation relies upon a neutral element for meaningful relationship: degrees of Depth and Height for Composition. The matter stands that as frequency rates the terms 'fast' or 'slow' are inadequate. Why? Basic form for meaning, as we have implied, demands spatial consideration. Psychovisualists assert that Depth-

and-Height, having no reality among noises, tones, pitches, no position in objective space, is exactly the necessity that makes systematized sounds as an independent phenomenon absurd, for Depth-and-Height, borrowed concept from the 'real' or objective world, is SEEN visually out of the boundaries of the eyes which are productive of a VISUAL FIELD. So conditioned is the psyche by the eye's command of a 'real' or material world of objects, so conditioned is it also by the neural response of our physical conditioning, that form comprehension psychically demands that we apply the same or the greater portion of such conditions to our thinking or it is meaningless. Therefore, notes are 'high' or 'low', soprano *above* bass, not because soprano is *above* bass, but because they have been given such spatial positions to which any deviation can refer for related meaning. Consciousness of a spatial relationship of form-significance derives from or IS visual perception.

A form of visualizing is 'SEEING IN THE MIND' or 'MIND'S EYE' or PSYCHOVISUAL. This has been described as difficult to trust or understand. A psychovisualist cannot accept this as difficult in any way. Yet it is commonly claimed that 'music uplifts our hearts, our minds,' etc., or one hears of 'cerebral music' or any number of references to 'thought,' 'intelligence,' etc., all of which involves Mind. Whatever the constitution of this something 'Mind,' be it from an Idealist or Materialist standpoint, generally, it is acceptable to both positions that enough 'quantitative substantiation' exists to warrant the term 'psychic phenomena.' The psychovisualist, in spite of whatever may be said in defense or in detraction of either position, is inclined to believe that the image making process is capable of a substantial influence on thinking. Dreams, wholly visible in 'mind' have a vivid existence thoroughly convincing during sleep. There is a possibility (and I do not need to inform of the varied theories regarding this) that a waking state with its irritabilities could easily obscure these 'psychic phenomena.' Such a direct physical phenomenon as sound, violently on the nerves, is substituted as all-important without the listener realizing that it is quite secondary to what really occurs when listening to music.

THE NATURE OF OBJECT-FORM IN COMPOSITION

The Academies instruct a student to regard sound, superstitiously, as an influence on the composing faculties, and as a phenomenon having a semantical and syntaxical structure depending upon, perhaps, 'authority' under which the composer must abide. A psychovisualist rejects this theory. Sound is auxiliary. Objects in composition primary. To hear a sound when no object is present immediately propounds the question, 'What made that noise?' THERE IS NO SOUND OR RHYTHM SAVE THAT PRODUCED BY OBJECTS IN (INERTIAL) CONFLICT OR 'MOTION.'

'Music,' so-called, has no privileged phenomena to bring into being. Sound is plastic in its methods and concrete in its expression. A purpose of every art is to be seen for comprehension and comprehended for the pleasure of the 'feeling' of relationships: a feeling interpreted as 'emotion' in the 'music.'

Therefore the figurative in 'music' may be that which refers to it as being 'heard'; for in any phase of the 'musical' vocabulary, visual images are employed; images that have in inception been of images received of images upon the eye. Chord 'color,' 'form,' 'architecture,' frequently employed words in 'musical' discussion among musicians, are distinctly indebted to visual phenomena and by the specified nature of the applications, signify some PARTICULARLY VISIBLE SOUND.

Here, of course, the psychovisualist can only more clearly discern divided essences of composition and sound application and language.

He grants that in common with painting and with sculptures and with language, 'music' has an identical purpose: communication. Notwithstanding, he feels that any effort to commit composition and sound applied completely over into the province of logic as behaving in language with the idea that such a province is the more related one, is the wrong perspective altogether. He feels, then, that such a relationship has been forced by figurative error and subtly influences to the point of being almost taken literally.

It needs then reaffirmation: Composition-and-sound literally is no language and cannot achieve what language can achieve in the way of communication by methods of discursion.

The specific application of words enables them to traverse in seconds a meaningfulness that a Composition-and-Sound must convey in a far greater time length and less specifically. Because of the specific object behind words, they enjoy a conceptual multiplication and manipulation that sound cannot logically emulate to the same effect.

Therefore the related art behind Composition more aptly is that of the painter, and achieves by various devices specification as nearly as possible to the word-noun-object. The word 'house' carries with it its spelling and its reference and, regardless to what use it is put, it maintains its identity as representative of a specific thing. A compound motivic organization acts similarly throughout a psychovisual composition in a presentational way. A composition and terms of sound has the disadvantage of having no semantics particularly applicable to specific things and must, so to speak, CREATE AND ESTABLISH (IN TERMS OF 'MOTION'-DEPTH-HEIGHT) AS CONCRETE AN OBJECT-FORM FOR ATTENTION AS POSSIBLE, keeping considerately in mind the dissipation of object identity in the delicate apparatus of (inertially) contradictory images.

It is this necessity, the establishment of an object form for attention, that Composition must achieve. And since that object-form in sound cannot be a majority symbol (as the noun 'house') of the thing, it can only do the next best thing; adopt the geometry of abstract form — a majority symbol.

Thus the psychovisualist composes with this attitude: that object-form in Composition and sound application is a synthesis of the ASSOCIABLE FLEXIBILITY of a WORD-NOUN-OBJECT IN LANGUAGES and the STATIC FORM-OBJECT IN PAINTING. Such a primary in psychovisual compositions is a 'COMPOUND MOTIVIC ORGANIZATION' or OBJECT-FORM.

The purpose, then, of Composition-and-Sounds is to be SEEN psychovisually and 'heard' only intermittently, finally not to be 'heard,' but COMPREHENDED by a feeling of relationships in object formations.

Sound is a result of the displaced elasticity of air caused by a moving body. From the valve compression of a horn, the frictional displacement of a violin string, we have the action of a body that generates sound.

If the body generating the sound is not seen or cannot be closely discerned in the immediate vicinity of the sound we engender the illusion of a thing without encumbrance: a kind of absolute, so to speak, a 'sound' FOR 'music' wherein the mechanical displacements of types leave us with a variety of proportionately small noises of different quality.

Congruent, these small dissimilar noises achieve a 'disembodied totality' or a separateness from the source. Composers who are not psychovisual accept this disembodied sound for music and employ it in 'movement' without the wholly indispensable formulation of a body, and yet illogically assuming 'movement' (illusory or otherwise) as possible without a body-form, proceed to compose in a state of psychic paradox exactly the opposite from the true state of affairs: that is, that a body or OBJECT-FORM MUST EXIST IN THE MIND OF THE COMPOSER BEFORE SOUND APPLIED AND BE SIMULTANEOUS WITH MOVEMENT OF ANY KIND IN COMPOSITION. It is assumed somehow that because the eye cannot directly observe the pressure vicinity of the frictional body on the air's elasticity, that sound without a body-form can be made to make sense that way. This is no better than saying that a perfectly fantastic object, never having been seen of heaven or earth, making a sound, but not present would make itself intelligible by that sound alone. To repeat: a sound heard and no object present invites the question, 'What made that noise?' It is that 'What' that Composition must achieve through sound applied: a distinct enough presentation of 'objects' or 'things' in motion and relationship; for there can be no such thing as meaningful form-significance in organized sound for the ear. Sounds must derive directly or indirectly of presentational objects in VISUAL FIELDS.

The psychovisual composer experiences that the metavisual sound (produced by displacements of elasticity, not of themselves sufficiently proportionate to a sound totality), this whole sound becomes on the psychic level an object of Forms of four Form Fields by stimulating visual properties in the psychic processes that are of meaningful space significance. It does on a psychic level what is being done on a physical level: demand inertial geometry of figural displacements.

(This brings us prematurely to a version of cosmic-equivalent inertia as an explanation of psychic displacements producing in a localised area illusions of motions, physically maintaining meanwhile, an elastic field of immobility.) (See Inertial Lineage Behind Psychic Content).

THE INVALIDITY OF INTERVALS-AS-SOUND, OF MELODY, OF HARMONY, FOR OBJECT-FORM

To say the word 'music' has persistently upheld a more intentional frame of sound succession than in evidence in noises. Having such a frame then must be at least intended for 'composition' however vague or unpsychovisual. The extent to which such a frame not only stems from intervals-as-sound, but refers to intervals-as-sound, to that extent it is not intentional. The more intentional the frame of order, the more is there Composition. The more Composition involved, the less the influence of sounds. In short, the most intentional framework for sound as applied on the part of a composer, is that of Composition. Intervals-as-sound in nature is the most unintentional framework, objective to the composer. The degree of maturity of a piece of 'music' is in its distance from unintentional intervals-as-sound toward Composition. Intervalic manipulation as Composition is, of course, a halfway mark.

There are music makers seriously convinced that intervalic manipulation imparts unity to a composition, and they concentrate upon this doubtful aspect and renounce sequential units as too primitive a mode for expression. They elaborate a set of intervals contrapuntally—retrograde, inverted, etc.—and the thought or expression, such as it is, in IN THE INTERVALS-AS-SOUND. The gigantic fallacy of such an interpretation of composition is evident. A third up, a fourth down, a minor second up, say for example, is strewn throughout a 'composition' with the expressive intention of an amoeba. The 'idea' is then said to have been 'developed' in the best manner of these dubious appellations. Actually it is aimless repetition of another more insidious sort. When the work is heard, it is a suffusion of sound; the so-called variety in unity depending on the listener's 'ear.' That 'ear,' if it is 'keen,' is treated (after considerable laborious exercise to unravel the composer's complications) to what? The extremely exciting repetition of intervals, 'ideas'? Inverted, retrograde, in dimunition, etc., and that with a host of intervalic overtones that no composer can control?

A psychovisualist wonders then, what novelty is there in a fifth or sixth, et al.—intervals centuries old and commonplace—that they are given so little to do besides be themselves? To a psychovisualist intervals-as-sound have value only when rhythmically forged into a compound motivic organization as object-form as a symbol, even a slogan, in notation; its purposes do not concentrate coherency on that limited level. Coherency occurs on the psychic level: that is, psychovisually. Contrarily, the chief meaningfulness in intervalic manipulation 'music' is but one limited level: notation. Notationally, there is a paradox: the most complex intervalic manipulation and counterpoint as 'composition,' when heard, may sound naive and pointless to the verge of imbecility: the simplest devices of notation and rhythm (psychovisually conducted, especially) may emerge as startlingly complex to hear. The latter is so because if psychovisually conducted, it can be understood only through visuality. The former will seem as it does because there is nothing for the 'mind' once the ear has performed its mechanical function well.

There is then no correlation between intervals-as-sound and form to justify intervalic manipulation as form discursively or otherwise. Intervals-as-sound could influence composition only if they themselves had to be composed, that is, given partials of relationship independent of nature. Intervalic tone-systems of yesterday and of today bear this responsibility. Unfortunately, as implied earlier in this piece, this leads to reversal of the creative process in composing. Various orders of sound arrangement exist, but they are for themselves and post themselves anterior to Composition consequently dictating to it their limited, even deplorable, terms. As previously explained, psychovisuality is Composition anterior to and formulative of harmonic technique, such as is necessary. Truthfully, such techniques are figurative, having very little validity for Composition. What validity there is, is in applications. As application to Composition, having no validity as form, their validity is intervalic sound-order as color. Limited space, however, prohibits a discussion of intervals-as-sound as harmonic color.

Intervals-as-sound, and color mentioned (one indicative of a lack of validity in Composition) a third condition of intervals demands examination: pitch relationship as time-space. Concerning time-space in Composition, a psychovisualist propounds his question: 'Why bother to conceive of "intervals" at all?' As time-space intervals they are of no matter as color. As time-space their pitch relationship as sound is transformed by 'high and low.' Their function in Composition as time-space returns us promptly to organization of 'high and low' as psychovisuality. Psychovisuality does not accept the validity of intervals-as-sound as melody. Tones sounded separately (melodic) of different pitch; tones of different pitch sounded simultaneously (harmonic) form relative volumic relationships out of intensity and dynamics. The compositional value of 'harmony' and 'melody' is identical in action: a continuum in two dimensional psychovisuality. The psychovisualist construes harmony, melody, as spurious terms and prefers to eradicate them conceptually. The opening note of a Composition, to a psychovisualist, is conceived not as sound, for there are no sounds in Composition, but as a point of attention from which a line will form becoming object-form. Such a condition for germination was described in terms of a tonic, soundfully.

The psychovisually intuitive composers of yesterday's

surprising heresies, relative to their day, seem less so if it is believed that the tonic may have represented something to them other than sound. Their sometimes violent departures in sound from their contemporaries intimate that they were very possibly not thinking in terms of sound, but in terms of space, points from which psychic structures evolved. A fixed point requires only another such point to become a potential of object-form in the four levels of fields to be discussed later.

To the psychovisualist, definitely, a sound establishing itself and joined by another sound establishes an attention-form for psychovisuality. It may be called a 'lineal.' The listener may take exception to this as he pleases, but a composer is risking coherency to do likewise.

Now obviously, the slightest so-called 'movement' (a successive coming through the ear of various pitches) annuls itself motionally (inertial contradiction) becoming a volumic continuum which psychic processes search for visual organization. From this point it is easy to conceive that every additional point must quickly formulate some contour of geometrical design, that is an object-form. The contradictions, so difficult of analysis in 'melodic' motional inertia (to be discussed later in illusory motion) pose these psychovisual problems: (1) That when a Composition is first 'heard,' the very incompatibility of HEARING A COMPOSITION poses a paradox which requires violent mental adjustment. We are not binaurally or psychically constituted to HEAR COMPOSITION. Composition must be SEEN. The phenomenal condition of senses, created obviously without considering 'music' as 'ordered sound' does what it is conditioned to do. (2) Consequently, NO COMPOSITION IS 'HEARD' WHILE IT IS LISTENED TO. Instead, the psychic processes, on the first hearing undergo a strenuous battery of successive sounds which, even as they fall on the ear, are not always 'heard,' for thought is engaged in visual reconstruction the very moment that seriously intended comprehension is put forth. This accounts for misunderstanding after a first hearing: the necessity for 'hearing' a composition many times before plausible visual comprehensibility, and lastly something that may answer some of a very elusive question, the question of the 'immortality' of a work. In regard to this last, sounds-for-composition-to-be-seen, being a thing which, partly by its contradictory nature, partly because of the unrealized proportionately small intake, plus the lack of materiality of volume form lines and the unpredictable character of 'memory' as 'PERSISTENCE OF VISION,' takes time.

BRIEF ANALYSIS OF THE INERTIAL LINEAGE BEHIND PSYCHIC CONTENT

Now there must be introduced seemingly irrelevant matter in a discussion of Composition and sound. However, psychovisual composition necessitates the answering of some philosophical questions.

Let it be understood that a psychovisualist does not present himself as a psychologist or scientist or philosopher, but is pressed usually to explain premises. That is, the mind-forms, the theatre of mind content of paramount consequence to psychovisual composition, becomes relevant by giving some account to the following hypothetical generalizations.

Thus far we have Object-Form in Composition which takes place in a qualitative substantive commonly called 'Mind.' If this seems a commonplace statement, that is, that it is common knowledge that 'music' takes place in 'mind,' this very assumption constitutes the basis of psychovisualism; for while this is certainly believed to be the case, very little 'music' is taught or 'composed' these days as if it were so.

As 'Music' was dedicated to church necessities or under the influence of noble houses under church influence, sounds as pre-composition took on certain standardizations. Even as far back as the Greeks, the modes had taken on associations. Plato, in the *Republic,* was apt to be disparaging of the effects of music on manhood, signifying the Dorian mode as possibly the better for its martiality. Legislations concerning music's demoralizing influence were put before the state.

As harmony solidified major and minor patterns, mood associations and religio-philosophical attitudes toward the representation of moral dispositions solidified. 'Evil' or 'unpleasant' or 'sad' thoughts overcome by 'good' or 'pleasant' thoughts became the struggles of tensions between major and minor. Sevenths and ninths (symbolic, perhaps, of disturbance or difficulty, even 'evil') were rigidly controlled by their always being resolved.

Interaction between moral dualism and sound dualism grew, so that any composer excessively addicted to minor keys or dissonances unresolved. The second movement of the F minor quartet with its chromatic gloom was very likely shocking to many of Beethoven's contemporaries.

Such attitudes (to a psychovisualist) approximated a harmonic mind-form: Dualism.

Suddenly the 'mind' paradoxes (of continuums and evolutions) and the cosmic paradoxes became inextricable (scientific investigation, of course, being vastly responsible) and the ensuing generations became qualitatively more complex.

With dualistic-absolutism dethroned, the psychic attitude gave evidence that it was not only capable of but intolerant of, any but complex manipulation of, dualistic-neutralism (humanism (nineteenth century) is to be included). Numerical mind-form construction, one, two, and therefore three, assumed a surprising qualitative distinction of its own, something new, so to speak: a state of psychic contradiction accepted, at least temporarily, as a condition of life.

Unfortunately, limited space prohibits the mind-form graph, but that graph was to show generally that mind-form has progressed away from simplified relationships and is capable of further progression as far as 'mind' is concerned. But the ear! Sound depending on the ear cannot keep up. A twelve tone work, for instance, employs contrapuntal technique to forge the complexity it senses in modern mind-form. Unfortunately, it exceeds the limitations of the ear by being too intervallically complex to sustain any reference to a composer's expression through the ear and at the same time be able to fulfill psychic necessities. In short, counterpoint is a retrogressive, even naive, way of seeking to represent the complexity of modern mind-form. Reasons why this is so have been given. Sound is secondary and cannot emulate of itself the important features of psychic phenomena. There could be possibly a row series in psychovisual units. The threat, however, to maintaining key avoidance would increase, which would greatly annoy an atonalist, conditioned as he is, seemingly more than anybody, to thinking in terms of sounds.

To the psychovisualist, it seems that the mind-forms have achieved a relationship to each other that sound cannot represent and so it must be abandoned as an object of Composition.

Mind-form having achieved this paradox of dualistic neutralism by conceiving of the probable resolution (something monistic), still acting dually, but knowing this, antithetically, three, there is by contemporary standards this fourth. This fourth is the psychic attitude to which progress has come.

Involved, of course, is spatial identity by 'instinct,' so to speak, for equivalences: a link between visual form comprehensions that might be described as neuropsychospatial visuality phenomenization by using sound.

To a psychovisualist, the psychic processes must be believed to be qualitatively substantive, but of a form of inertial identity struggles.

PSYCHOVISUAL INERTIA HYPOTHESIS

Two spatial opposites, each qualitatively substantive, together in given space form third different from themselves. A three-formation distinct. (Three-form borrowing distinction by subtraction from opposites.) Three-form achieves fourth distinction (force of being in place of three resisting tendency to withdraw from constitutional identity). This fourth inertial cannot be analyzed actually, existing in the comparisons. Its potential: presentation three-four form.

This essay, originally published in 1955, concludes with the following note: "To be discussed in future issues of *Free Lance*: Four Form Fields of Psychovisual Composition as Presentational Three-Four Form; Composing Illusory Motion; Persistence of Vision Limitations as Counterpoint." In 1958, Atkins would follow up with "Psychovisual Perspective for 'Musical' Composition in *Free Lance* vol. 5, no. 1. A pdf of this much longer discussion will be made available to readers on the Unsung Masters website.

Russell Atkins has said that the original publication of this text contained several errors, introduced by the student typesetters. To that end, obvious and distracting errors in punctuation have been corrected. Atkins' idiosyncratic use of capital letters, however, has been retained in this version of the essay.

Death Is Only Natural

Evie Shockley

Russell Atkins' baroque idiosyncrasies and ghastly preoccupations have rightfully focused the few critics who have treated his poetry thus far on its innovative and gothic qualities. I'd like to promote an additional lens through which to examine his work—not to supplant these approaches, but to expand or recalibrate them. I suggest we think of Atkins as a nature poet as well. Aldon Nielsen's groundbreaking work on Atkins' oeuvre shines a spotlight briefly on its "characteristic . . . linking of the world of the 'natural' to the mediations of the 'cultural'" (51). Picking up with Nielsen's insight, I propose we foreground the omnipresence of "nature"—which is to say, the elements of the world we place in opposition to manmade structures and systems—in Atkins' imaginary, and begin working through its implications for not only Atkins' writing but also the various traditions within which his writing can be read.

Approaching Atkins' poetry with an eye towards his interest in nature reveals it to be as definitive a characteristic of his work as his syntactic twists and deliberately anachronistic diction. His collections are bursting with pieces that describe the seasons, the weather, the way the light changes over the course of the day, or the interactions of animals.

The very titles of his poems convey this preoccupation: "A Winter's Walk," "Lake in a Storm," and the typographically fabulous "NIGH)Th'CRY,PT." It may be helpful to think of the ways nature functions in his poetics as falling into three categories—perhaps because, as he says of his infamous "apostrophe 'd'" usage, its "properties strike out simultaneously and three-dimensionally!" ("Preface" n.p.). First, he sometimes presents us with textbook examples of the pathetic fallacy (in the sense in which John Ruskin originally used the term in *Modern Painters*), depicting the natural environment in ways that communicate the speaker's emotional response to an intensely charged situation—for Atkins, this often means fraught social conditions. For instance, in "Four of a fall," Atkins delivers the dark, tumultuous autumn weather as a counterpart of the speaker's despair over a friend's drug dealing and addiction:

> He was one night grim statued at my door.
> He came to sell. One in the grey
> who took the lamps down, lay in wait,
> spider'd across, adder'd among.
> It turned to storm, a mad tear up.
> An ominous of rain shuddered from a banged sky.
> A flight of lightnings
> Swift'd terribly across. (14)

His poems in this category recall the Graveyard Poets of 18th-century England and the Romantic poetry that their work prefigured, using nature symbolically (spiders, snakes, and storms carrying their usual cultural freight) to magnify the horrors that his friend's behaviors represent for the speaker. Such poems comprise, in large part, Atkins' closest tie to the gothic tradition.

In other poems, nature is the central actor in its own drama. One of his most stylistically unconventional poems, "Night and a distant church," uses innovative typography to enhance the connection between sonic and visual representations of nature. The second stanza of the poem, written in 1950, appears in this still unusual form:

```
upon
the mm
            mm
wind mmm m
      mmm
into the mm wind
rain now and again
the mm
            wind
      ells
b
        ells
     b
```

Humans recede into the background, our presence marked only by the sounds we send out to play in the sky with the natural elements. Atkins' control of his medium is amazing in this poem, which uses visual placement of language—or, at least, letters—to indicate passage of time (how long the wind's moans continue), intervals of sound (deep notes answered by somewhat higher ones as the clapper strikes each side of the bell), and movement through space (the sound of the bells drifting away and even, perhaps, the falling rain), all at once.

The third dimension, so to speak, of nature's properties in Atkins' poetry lies between the first two—that is, the human world and the natural world meeting in a more balanced or reciprocal relationship. With nature neither decorating human interactions nor eclipsing them, in these poems Atkins indicates how interdependent and overlapping nature and culture are, while exploring a wide variety of natural environments and social subjects. "Lakefront,

Cleveland," from his volume *Heretofore* (not to be confused with the entirely different poem with exactly the same title in the collection *Here in The*), is a terrific example of this category of work. The piece presents us with the fact of an abortion and the speaker's encounter with the evidence of it: "a jellied foetus" that has passed through the sewage system and washed up as "pulp," in "a murmur of laps," on the shore of what is presumably Lake Erie (30). The speaker offers no judgment of the woman who has "secreted her burden / . . . in her toilet"—a wonderful phrase that encompasses both the physicality of the abortion process and the necessarily clandestine character of this operation in 1954, when the poem was composed. Though such words as "extremed" and "excruciation" suggest a sympathetic construction of her condition (before, during, and after the procedure), the poem is focused on the lakefront scene, where Atkins places us at the intersection of life and death. The penultimate stanza captures the tensions between these two great forces and, similarly, between the demands of the social world and the power of the natural world:

> Now, then, God, listen: I'd swear
> I heard, heard low,
> its sigh-sounds lapse
> as from furious determination—
> furious, horrid determination!
> Though stretch cast out night's long;
> though hideous voyaged afar;
> though there was extremed
> wake of the city;
> though there's excruciation
> under sepulchral sky;
> though there is grave's after
> and grave's before, I heard
> I swear, some of furious determination— (31)

Though the poem can be read in terms of the two binaries I've named, they complicate—rather than reinforce—one another. Perhaps the woman's "furious determination" to survive the difficult circumstances of her life leads to the foreclosure of the (potential) life of the fetus. This struggle, which begins in the city, ends on the lakefront, painted here as a funereal environment comprising both nocturnal gloom and ecological degradation. There, the speaker is the sole audience for the similarly "furious determination" of the fetus and the increasingly polluted lake, each of whose "will to live," if you will, is tied to the other's in the poem by the "sigh-sounds" that are implicitly attributed to the former, but in fact produced by the latter (the "murmur of laps" returning?). These irresolvable tensions are replicated within the speaker as conflicting emotions, and the poem closes on the image of him responding to the moment "with a laugh of a cry!" (31).

Atkins falls within a small but significant cluster of formally innovative African American poets whose poetry is centrally concerned with exploring the human condition through or as nature. Such poets as Anne Spencer, Ed Roberson, and Will Alexander, about whom I have written elsewhere, have produced work that demands that we expand the concept of "nature poetry" (and that of "political poetry," for that matter) to include poems that broach heretofore excluded issues of race and gender in such settings as gardens, wilderness, and interplanetary space. To these poets, I would add C. S. Giscombe (who grew up in Dayton) and, especially, Julie Patton, who is, like Atkins, a native of Cleveland and whose work is particularly invested in ecology and ecopoetics, per se. In a beautiful and incisive introduction to the journal *Crayon*'s 1999 feature on Atkins' poetry, she emphasizes the role of place, geographically and culturally, in the literature produced by a whole raft of talented and acclaimed black Ohioans:

> In the *citta invisibles* of northeast Ohio, where the agrarian world meets the urban industrial, northern meets southern culture, "underground railroad" meets "promised land," and lake encounters sky, I locate Russell Atkins in another continuum—one related to my own preoccupation with the poetics of place and curiosity about why this particular region, and the state it dissolves itself in, generated so many ground-breaking American writers of African descent—a sense of time, space, surface, and rupture often articulated in the writings of Toni Morrison (Lorain), Rita Dove (Akron), Adrienne Kennedy (Cleveland . . .), Thylias Moss (Akron), and other former Clevelanders, . . . [including] Langston Hughes, whose blues can also be traced to Lake Erie rhythms. ("Hear In The" 2)

I exchanged emails with Patton about Atkins, and she underscored the impact of the landscape and climate of Cleveland, in particular, upon his work (and her own): "Place, a sense of being, in that place, is what comes thru. You can hear those almost metal tones, burnished by trees and water, escape routes and plain day. If you could get past the clouds. They had their own ships due north" (Patton). This racialized landscape importantly informs Atkins' poetry, manifesting perhaps as a need to "escape" poetic convention, more often than as an explicit interrogation of race.

Atkins' consistent attention to death and recurring portrayals of dark and stormy nights in his poems distinguishes him among the group of African American nature poets I've set forth here—though his gothic vision of nature might be seen as the "dark" side of the same Romantic coin that Anne Spencer's garden images draw upon. But both he and Spencer diverge from Romanticism in ways that connect them to Roberson, Patton, and Alexander—as well as a wider, multiracial group of ecopoets including Brenda Iijima,

Jack Collum, Cecilia Vicuña, and Juliana Spahr—in their recourse to unconventional formal techniques to get at the nuances and challenges of their understanding of nature.

Though Atkins' particular brand of unconventionality, at its most distinctive, can be off-putting to readers unfamiliar with his work, it is worth stressing that its strangeness is at heart a means of communicating the commonness, the quotidian nature of death. Like night, like winter, death is always coming—but unlike these cyclical phenomena, it can be very unpredictable. Thus, in Atkins' poetry, as domesticated an article as coffee is implicitly refigured as a means of staving off death, insofar as caffeine counters our bodies' inevitable flagging each evening, from "seventy-five rpm down to thirty-three" ("Coffee"). The result of this winding down is described in syntax as circular as the vinyl records playing on the machine:

> that there isn't
> going to be anything else
> seems for sure, is the night,
> seems forever'd

But just when we think we've accepted the journey from morning to inescapable night, he reminds us that death can come without warning. The unpredictable death is still quotidian—"[h]ere in the newspaper," that daily dose of anxiety—but for those death claims—in a train wreck, in this instance—it arrives quite suddenly, violently, and unannounced ("It's here in the"). Atkins reckons with this disturbing contrast by presenting, in turn, a contrast between the ugliness of death and the twisted beauty of the poem that tells of it, a time-honored poetic strategy, revitalized through the insistent musicality and grim, corkscrewy humor of his language. I'll close with his poem's closing images, which both provide and resist closure:

Something of a full stop of it
crash of blood and the still shock
            of stark sticks and an immense swift gloss
And two dead no 's lie aghast still
One casts a crazed eye and the other's
      closed dull
              the heap twists up
      hardening the unhard, unhardening
      the hardened

Works Cited

Atkins, Russell. "Coffee." *Here in The.* Cleveland: Cleveland State U Poetry Center, 1976. 41.

—. "Four of a fall." *Heretofore.* London: Paul Breman, 1968. 12-15.

—. "It's here in the." *Here in The.* Cleveland: Cleveland State U Poetry Center, 1976. 47.

—. "Lakefront, Cleveland." *Heretofore.* London: Paul Breman, 1968. 30-31.

—. "Preface." *Juxtapositions.* Cleveland: Russell Atkins, 1991. N. pag.

—. "Night and a distant church." *Heretofore.* London: Paul Breman, 1968. 10.

Nielsen, Aldon. *Integral Music: Languages of African American Innovation.* Tuscaloosa: U of Alabama P, 2004.

Patton, Julie. "Hear In The." *Crayon* 2 (1999): 1-4.

—. "Re: Russell Atkins." Message to the author. 4 Sept. 2012. E-mail.

Russell Atkins: "Heretofore"

Aldon Lynn Nielsen

"I did not want to be "Well-Rounded."
Russell Atkins ("Russell Atkins," 7)

At a time when the dating of even so broadly studied a phenomenon as the Harlem Renaissance remains a subject of torrid debate, few would care to supply a date for the heretofore little noted emergence of an identifiable avant-garde among African American poets. Still, the breaking of some rigidities is worthy of rereading. Even before the first poems bearing the signature of LeRoi Jones began to appear in small press magazines around the country, Russell Atkins had established himself as a prominent advocate of avant-garde poetics in America. Atkins published his first poems when he was only eighteen years old and, according to Casper LeRoy Jordan's afterword to Atkins' 1961 collection *Phenomena*, Atkins' characteristic devices and ideas "were in effect" as early as 1946-50 in poems that circulated in magazines such as *Experiment, View, Beloit Poetry Journal* and others. Jordan remarks that "A perusal of poetry publications in which Mr. Atkins' poetry appeared reveals that he remained one of the very few consistently experimental poets" (76). In the author's biography that accompanies Atkins' fullest collection of his life's work in verse, *Here in The*, the poet is quoted as stating, "I was avant garde before I knew there was an avant garde" (52). While too many current-day critics still evidence no awareness that there has been an African American avant-garde in America, Atkins was an active and recognized force for experimental poetics across a span of four decades. Early champions of his work included Carl Van Vechten, Langston Hughes, Parker Tyler, Charles Henri Ford, and Marianne Moore, and he has been one of the most prolific black experimentalists in American literature, publishing more than ten books along with numerous articles, notes and dramatic pieces contributed to little magazines here and abroad. (An even earlier supporter was Atkins' Latin teacher at Cleveland's Central Junior High, Helen Chesnutt, daughter of Charles Waddell Chestnutt.) Atkins was a mainstay of *Free Lance*, which Conrad Kent Rivers once called "The oldest black-bossed magazine around" (quoted in Redmond, 328), and which the editors of *Black American Literature Forum* described as "the longest and continuously published black journal" (Atkins, "Dumas," 159).

Atkins did receive a degree of recognition for his tireless and highly individual efforts. He was a frequent reader on the poetry circuit, reading at universities, galleries and coffee houses around the country, and he was invited to both the Bread Loaf and Iowa writers' workshops. Atkins was awarded an honorary doctorate from Cleveland State University and was for a time the writer in residence at Cuyahoga Community College. Karamu House, where Atkins taught creative writing for more than a decade, produced a "Tribute to Russell Atkins" in 1971 featuring performances and critical discussions of his works in music and literature. Dudley Randall, of Broadside Press fame, journeyed from Detroit to join in that retrospective evening, presenting a reading from Atkins' correspondence. At other times, members of the Cleveland Orchestra performed his "Objects" for cello, violin and piano. Composer Hale Smith wrote his "In Memoriam" based on a poem by Atkins, and

Stefan Wolpe introduced Atkins' "Psychovisual Perspective for 'Musical' Composition" at the Darmstadt Festival of Contemporary Music in 1956. Atkins' work in music theory is cited by H.H. Stückenschmidt in his 1969 study, *Twentieth Century Music*. Marianne Moore was sufficiently taken with Atkins' poem "Trainyard at Night" that she read it as part of a WEVD radio broadcast in New York as early as 1951. (The poem was subsequently reprinted in Atkins' Breman Heritage book, *Heretofore*.) In July of that year Moore wrote to Atkins saying that she had mutilated and mangled the reading of his poem, despite an earlier, successful rehearsal. She reported to Atkins that despite her reading she had heard quite good reactions to the poem from her listeners, concluding that it had been the distinctive element of the broadcast (Moore, 7/14/51).

When *Free Lance* published a special issue in tribute to Atkins' career in 1970, the issue's editorial commentaries, written by Casper LeRoy Jordan and J. Stefanski, placed Atkins' experimental works against a background in which "Conservatism dominated contemporary American poetry through the early fifties." They proceed to argue that "In spite of a highly visible attempt to deny the fact. Atkins has been among the most subtle influences of the last two decades" (1). Elsewhere in the issue they term Atkins' poem "Night and a Distant Church" "the masterpiece of 'concretism'" (9) and "the most exquisitely suggestive 'concrete' piece of the last twenty years" (8). They credit Atkins with having published some of the first examples of concrete verse in the United States, and they argue that "the bridge between typographical and 'concrete' is difficult to define until one knows of Atkins' ingenious combination of elevated tone and meticulous application of device to thought and subject" (8). Given the occasion of a tribute, some overstatement (perhaps even a misplaced modifier or two) can be forgiven. It would probably be difficult, though, for literary historians to prove the "high visibility" of attempts (by critics or by Atkins himself) to deny Atkins' importance and influence, but he has indeed been omitted from almost all histories of American literature in general and American poetic experimentalism in particular. It is somewhat easier to point to published attempts to deny the importance of African American literature in toto, stretching from Thomas Jefferson through Allen Tate, and the general ignorance attributable in part to the legacy of that history of racism. Despite Atkins' valuable exchanges of correspondence with Charles Henri Ford, Parker Tyler, Marianne Moore, Carl Van Vechten and Edith Sitwell, the published histories of the movements from Modernism to Postmodernism have not yet found reason to mention Atkins, and despite his early associations with Langston Hughes, the critical efforts to recover important black writers who have been overlooked have yet to renew the reputation of Russell Atkins. (A herald can be seen, though, in the special section devoted to Atkins in a more recent issue of the small press magazine *Crayon.*)

In part, this critical invisibility can be blamed upon a too widespread tendency among academic critics to ignore small press publications until such time as an author has achieved a modicum of public critical interest. With the exception of his 1976 collected poems *Here in The,* which was published by Cleveland State University's Poetry Center, and his chapbook in Paul Breman's Heritage Series, published in London, Atkins' books were all limited editions from small avant-garde presses. Roughly half of his books were printed by Free Lance Press, and others were brought out by Cleveland's Renegade Press and California's Hearse Press. As a result, the volumes *Here in The* and *Heretofore* are the only collections among Atkins' works that are likely to be found in many research libraries, and they were also the only books of his readily obtainable in literary book stores, so long as they remained in print. But far more than this, Atkins' critical invisibility is likely the result of the combination of the nature of his writing and his identity as a black experimentalist. Though it has often proved difficult for white authors of avant-garde texts to get published, enormously difficult in fact, and while it has often taken a very long time indeed for critics to come around to the reading of such works, we do now have a body of critical studies available to students of such Modernists as Mina Loy, Gertrude Stein and Louis Zukofsky, and the critical bibliographies surrounding the texts of such contemporary poets as Clark Coolidge, Susan Howe and Charles Bernstein are thickening appreciably. Still even though collections of Atkins' papers have been on deposit for some time at Atlanta University and at the Chicago Public Library, Atkins remains, as Ronald Henry High notes in his article on the poet in the *Dictionary of Literary Biography,* "better known abroad than in America" (24). High concludes his entry by predicting that "as more people get familiar with Atkins, his approach to literary expression will be better appreciated and more fully understood. As his work is more performed and more read, as it garners more critical attention and documentation, his genius will come to be recognized in the United States as it is in Europe" (32). (A mark of Atkins' renown overseas is that the scholar of Neo-African culture Jahnheinz Jahn made a point of stopping to visit with Atkins during one of his trips from Germany [Simon, 8].) High made his predictions nearly thirty years ago. A check of the most recent Modern Language Association bibliographies yields few citations of critical work devoted to the study of Atkins' poetry.

As early as 1950, Russell Atkins, who by that time had been publishing poems in magazines for six years, was already known as a significant new talent among African American poets. When Langston Hughes guest-edited a special "Negro Poets Issue" of the magazine *Voices* in 1950, he included Atkins along with Waring Cuney, Owen Dodson, Robert Hayden, Melvin B. Tolson and Gwendolyn Brooks. By the next year Marianne Moore was introducing some of his most experimental work to New York radio audiences, and Atkins' commitment to his avant-garde stance seems never to have wavered since. Abby and Ronald Johnson, in their history of African American magazines, identify Atkins as "the most technically experimental" writer included in *Free Lance.* They go on to complain that "He was so experimental in both essays and poems that it was often difficult to trace his ideas" (157). They are not alone in their complaint. In his reply to Adelaide Simon's praises of Atkins' work in the special Cleveland issue of *Input* magazine in 1964, Kirby Congdon expresses his opinion that Atkins has done all in his power to deserve his public obscurity. Simon, who had worked as Atkins' co-editor at *Free Lance,* had written that "there is a great deal of sadness in the lack of critical acclaim for Russell Atkins' work in the very avant garde itself" (8). Congdon concedes that Atkins' ideas, the matter of his work, are original and provocative. It is the work's form and language that Congdon finds objectionable. Congdon claims that if Atkins has been neglected, "it is only because he chooses to write in a lush, archaic take-off of Shakespearean lingo that sounds great at first but does the author a disservice, since it comes off as pretentious and unnatural" (9). In the end, though, Congdon is not so much concerned about the disservice Atkins may be inflicting upon himself as he is about what he thinks Atkins is doing to his readers. As is all too often the case when a critic wishes to dismiss experimental poetics, Congdon accuses Atkins of writing this way in order to curry favor with critics (apparently without success). Congdon advises Atkins, "I am still hoping he will write for us readers & ... forget the students, explicators, and scholars whose interest he apparently wishes to capture." It would seem that no "lack of acclaim" from students and critics will ever be enough to protect a writer from this charge. As Congdon concludes, he states, suddenly adopting the royal first-person plural: "We don't think, though, that the sadness lies in our neglect of [Atkins]; but rather in his neglect of us," and the critic offers the poet, as a model to follow, translations of Robert Graves (9). Atkins has often, in his own critical comments scattered through successive issues of *Free Lance,* attacked this sort of legislating of the allowable in language and in form. "The 'authority,'" Atkins writes, is in the "teaching values racket" ("Of" 1963, 22). The authority has at his disposal an effective disciplinary apparatus. "Conferences, classrooms and magazines are his to cultivate the merely presentable poem for which he knows what 'techniques' are 'proper' and who is proper for them" (21-22). In that same collection of notes in 1963, Atkins, speaking of Robert Hayden, indicates his own acute awareness of the facts of life facing black poets in America. "It is not surprising in America," Atkins observes, "that we would hear less of an accomplished non-white poet, for it is bound up with ethnic obstacles in connection with the mainstream of literature in America (23).

Eugene Redmond's assessment at the end of his summary of Atkins' career in *Drumvoices* is both more measured and more fair than either Congdon's or that of the Johnsons, and is more temperate in its appreciations of Atkins than Simon could be about her co-editor. In Redmond's reading, "Once Atkins' technique is understood ... his poetry can be enjoyed for its witty, wacky, yet serious philosophical musings" (329). There is a central wackiness, it must be conceded, to Atkins' writing that should not be lost sight of even as we read his more convoluted critical essays, but it is a motivated wackiness. Sterling Brown frequently quipped to those of us who knew him in Washington, DC, that "any black man who isn't paranoid is crazy." As Russell Atkins worked his way through the madness of America's racialized languages, trying to make art out of discourses designed to deny his entry, he developed a characteristic mode of writing that, while it resembles some aspects of the works of his contemporaries in local instances, is finally unlike that of any other black writer of his time, perhaps unlike any writer of his time, perhaps unlike any writer of time. Always, though, he evidenced an ironic sensibility about his projects and his reception. He knew that some of his methods brought resistance from those committed to more traditional reading strategies, and he at times used more traditional writing strategies to comment upon that fact. Perhaps Kirby Congdon had never read Atkins' "Notes on Negro Poets," a 1954 poem composed after reading Hughes and Bontemps's *Poetry of the Negro*. The poem is anything but an example of "lush, archaic lingo," and few readers would have any difficulty making their way through its stanzas. One must, however, have read some of Atkins' more experimental forms in order to appreciate just how far into his cheek he has worked his tongue when he offers the following self-assessment:

> I cannot make heads or tails
> of the new poets among Negroes
> But then why bother?
> Could anything be made of them
> would it matter?
> But some say that they
> cannot make heads or tails
> of ME! How can that be?
> I am so clear! not like
> Gwendolyn Brooks—
> all blear.
>
> (16)

This from a poet who more frequently wrote lines like the following:

Clad of shrub shreds to rush
and for the exodus'd
difficult will snow.

(*Podium*, n.p.)

Juxtapaposing such lines as these to Atkins' humorous claims to clarity is not the revelation of a grand contradiction. We should, instead, understand that Atkins, like the early Objectivist poets, conceived of a clarity that differed substantively from the model offered by mainstream poetry at mid-century. None of the words Atkins uses in the second example of his verse sends readers scurrying for their dictionaries, and the only unusual word formation is his transformation of "exodus" into a past-tense verb through the use of an apostrophe (a technique used perhaps too frequently by Atkins—but in this instance I can't help hearing an intertextual echo of the "exodusters" in his line). Neither does Atkins' poem "Demolition," with its "clad of shrub," burden readers with extensive and opaque allusions (though both Euclid and Medusa get mentioned). What readers face here is a kind of formal opacity. Most readers are not used to encountering phrases like "Clad of shrub shreds to rush" in their daily experiences of language, even in verse, and so may tend to resist reading such phrases despite the fact that one can, and fairly quickly, begin to make a series of sensible readings out of the poem. What Atkins jokingly suggests is that his poems are at least as "clear" as those of his more celebrated contemporaries.

It is true that if we compare an Atkins line like "Clad of shrub shreds to rush" to some of the denser of Brooks's lines their poetics might appear somewhat less disjunct. In "The Second Sermon on the Warpland" Brooks writes:

Salve salvage in the spin.
Endorse the splendor splashes;
Stylize the flawed utility; (454)

In the face of such a passage (and it is important to recall that these lines occur in one of the poems Brooks wrote after she had begun communing with Don Lee and Sonia Sanchez), it may be hard to argue with Atkins' ironic assertions that his own poems are actually less "blear" than those of Brooks. His concluding stanza to "Eloge" might well pass as a fair imitation of the Brooks of the 1950s:

> Such seer ones who had
> no repose and to whom
> nothing trophied came,
> who strove to save the world
> I threnody them all
> remorse, for it is drear to tell
> how lacked is of them
> sculpture
>
> (27)

Only in the last two lines do we find the characteristic twist of those syntactic displacements that mark a poem as quintessentially Atkins. It is not that Atkins inhabited an entirely disparate poetic universe from Brooks and others of the time; the differences are matters of degree. (And Atkins is more likely to be up to mischief when he violates Modernist admonitions against poetic inversions of phrase grammar than is Brooks in her earlier works.) One effect of the sequestering of experimentalists like Atkins from the more recent genealogies of black verse has been that we are no longer able to see the continuum that stretches from the avant-garde of the 1950s and early 1960s to the more widely read and discussed later poems of a figure like Brooks.

Atkins wrote his "Notes on Negro Poets" several years before the younger Amiri Baraka published his controversial essay on "The Myth of a Negro Literature." In that

1962 speech, Baraka claimed that "Negro" literature had in the past been "a method or means of displaying ... participation in the 'serious' aspects of American culture" (*Home*, 108), and then went on to complain of some contemporary African American poets that they would "reject the gaudy excellence of 20th century American poetry in favor of disembowelled Academic models of second-rate English poetry, with the notion that somehow it is the only way poetry should be written" (113). Baraka would subsequently revise his reading of some earlier black authors, but his complaint was one that he had in common Atkins. The older poet's 1954 poem reaches a hilarious peak of racial punning when Atkins sighs, "Ah Negro poetry where perfect sham / is passing!" (16) The pun itself is one instance of Atkins' own gaudy excellence. This doubled figure, which also echoes a Melvillean "Ah, humanity," conjoins a complaint about the sham of passing mediocre and imitative verse as thought and the high art of poetry, and the sham of passing for white. To underscore his estimation of the banality of what he later was to call "the remaining Kipling zealots and the Paul Laurence Dunbars [and] the Tennysonians ..." (*Free Lance* 13.33), all those African American poets who rejected the new poetics of the postwar era, and even those of the Modernists, in preference for continued mining in the played-out vein of archaic verse forms, Atkins resorts to doggerel to record his ironic critiques. "I'll tell you when I'm crushed / by books—when I read / Gwendolyn Brooks!" Atkins exclaims in "Notes on Negro Poets" (17). Of a prominent voice from the Harlem Renaissance Atkins says: " When I think of Countee Cullen / I grow sullen" (17). As far as Atkins is concerned, Cullen should not have marveled that God would make a poet black and bid him sing. For Atkins, the really curious thing was that no one bade Cullen cease (a criticism that is ironically returned to Atkins by Congdon's later ripostes). Though Atkins would subsequently describe Robert Hayden's imagination as "freely decorative" and speak of his poetry as a "relief from an exaggerated preoccupation with 'Content'" ("Of' 1963, 23), here he writes: "How like the consummation of too much / Are the poem of Robert Hayden / With too many big words laden"(17).

It was what he saw as an "exaggerated preoccupation with content" on the part of critics as well as poets that most exercised Atkins in these "Notes." It was not that Atkins denied the political implications of literary art, nor that he refused politically oriented readings of poetry and poetics. To the contrary, he exhibited a sophisticated understanding of the culturally constructed nature of both race and prejudice, and of the role literature and literary education played in both the construction and defense of racial hegemony in the realm of culture. In 1964, ten years after he wrote his "Notes," the editors' column in *Free Lance* recorded "Some Thoughts Defining 'Mainstream' in Relation to 'Education' and Destructive Power." These later thoughts indicated Atkins' estimation of the role played by institutions of state power, such as education, in the naturalizing of hegemonic discourse, as well a his comprehension of the essentially arbitrary nature of signification:

> Educated prejudice—the most difficult of prejudice—is not based on ignorance, but upon "knowledge" that has been created and culturally adjusted under Military control. It is in command of enough information that it can usually refute arguments employed to convince it of something with arguments equally valid. Even should this fail it is aware of this: that in the real of semantics, abstraction, types of creativity, and on the plane of values, little can be proved to be other than arbitrary. (26)

Some thirty years later, what the American Media came to call the culture wars in education continued to rage over just these grounds. As poststructuralist theories, feminism, cultural studies, ethnic studies, new historicism, and even new poetries increasingly challenged mainstream education from within the institutions of education themselves, frequently issuing their challenges in terms much like those used in 1964 in *Free Lance*, the mainstream's cultural authorities and politicians like George H. W. Bush and William Bennett attempted, often with considerable militancy, to reassert control. As far as Russell Atkins and *Free Lance* colleagues could see, canon construction and publication are an integral force in the "military control" of cultural values. "Often enough," we read in *Free Lance*, "anthologies reveal or confirm or even determine a group's relationship to the 'mainstream' as defined above" (27). On this view, the critical preoccupation with the content of African American poetry is a means of determining, adjusting, perhaps even policing group identity and group subject positions. A mirroring preoccupation on the part of writers effectively sustains the assumptions and agendas of critical hegemony. As Atkins puts it in his "Notes," again turning humor against himself:

> Negroes, Freedom, etc., in poetry!
> (a word dear reader;
> they weary). Many frowns and all
> pass over them mysterious,
> and some die over them,
> and I—I've been so heroic—
> I've sighed over them.
>
> (16)

Atkins also recognized the intimate critical association in American thought between the preoccupation with the content of African American verse and the continuing demand for a "realism" of linguistic surface in the literary forms of black writing. As we've seen in Congdon's attacks on Atkins' style, as we can see in Sarah Webster Fabio's attacks on Melvin B. Tolson's language, and as we can see in Professor Joyce Ann Joyce's attacks upon black critics who make use of the language of poststructuralist theories, American criticisms of African American writing continue to posit an audience (always vaguely out there, somewhere, congregating in virtual ghettoes as "the people") befuddled by forms of English that purportedly could never be their own. (Interestingly, critics making this type of charge seldom present themselves as unable to comprehend the language under attack, though they do present themselves as "among the people"; it is always "the people" who will not be able to understand.) Such attitudes tried and tired Atkins, as did those "tea party" poets who thought of the poem as a therapeutic baring of the emotions. At the close of his "Notes on Negro Poets," Atkins condemns that conservative adherence to literary realism (not to be confused with "the real") that would again be condemned in the next decade by Amiri Baraka and Clarence Major:

> You know how sensitive I am and all
> and cannot bear writers ungeneral—
> Realists and so on? How they do bore!
> because there are not a few of them
> but a few more!
>
> (18)

Precious little of Atkins' poetry is written in this mode, though he is sometimes this precious. Atkins was having a good deal of fun matching the banality of form in his "Notes" to the mediocrity of technical accomplishment that passed among so many poets wedded to traditional forms. Always, Atkins wanted forms that suited his subjects. In his memorial poem to Langston Hughes, which is for the most part written in Atkins' more familiar syntactically disruptive style, the poet suddenly inserts a traditionally rhymed couplet in the manner of Hughes's best known poems. "May Twenty-Second, Nineteen Sixty Seven," included by Atkins in the 1967 Hughes memorial issue of *Free Lance,* is an elegy honoring that older poet who encouraged (and published) the wilder and younger experimentalist. "Few fugitives had been sheltered by him/ as had I" (23), Atkins remembers of the poet whose prefatory note had introduced the very first issue of *Free Lance.* Atkins rails against "eternal syndicates" That "won't dare countenance things free" (22), and contrasts them to Hughes, who whatever doubts he may have harbored about the more extreme formal revolutions of the next generation, was willing to lend his name and prominence to the idea of free verse experiment. In what has to be one of his most eloquent couplets, Atkins follows a citation from Hughes with lines in which his apostrophized verb forms seem more than usually "natural" and sound as if they were drawn from Hughes himself:

> "Ain't no sense in my being dead."
>
> They cannot prey on him: he left instead,
> Jazz'd in fire, funeral'd in red
>
> (21)

Atkins obviously rembers Hughes's written memory of the lyric, "Fire gonna burn my soul." Historically minded readers of this elegy will also remember, whether intended to or not, that decades earlier the magazine of experimental literature by young black writers that Hughes had helped to found, a forerunner of *Free Lance*, was titled *Fire.* Hughes recalled in later years that *Fire* represented a desire to "épater le bourgeois, to burn up a lot of the old stereotyped Uncle Tom ideas of the past" (18-19). That magazine was itself "funeral'd in red" when the bulk of the press run was immolated in a building fire (Johnson, 79). Having briefly adopted a Hughes-like diction and form, Atkins then immediately reverts to a language more his own, to those yet odder verb and noun forms that gave Kirby Congdon so much consternation. The metrics of Atkins' lines here remain traditional, but like John Ashbery, Atkins floats "normal" sounding sentences atop that measure that seem to float loose from normal modes of predication and subordination: "Which facts are worst to their abhor/ of the valuables, his, that I possess" (21).

Atkins often employs forms that hover close to the traditional, only to twist the direction of readerly expectations aroused by the generic cues offered by those forms. His particular mode of experiment took the history of genres (including the genre of the concrete poem) as the givens upon which he worked his improvisations. In the course of a *Free Lance* review in 1966. Atkins declared his belief that:

> A poet cannot change, for whatever purpose, the fundamental units of perception in terms of accents, trochees, ect., can only be permutated. American poets hint of a complete liberation from a tradition. However, they must employ that tradition's own devices, viz., syntactical logic, morphology, etc., compounded of words of "the latine & mo from the French and mo from the Italian—" according to one Renaissance purist. Regardless of the pros and cons of the dispute, any originality toward figurative effect through the English language may inescapably resemble that language's traditions at, say, the drop of a hat? ("Musophilus," 13)

One of the disarming things about Atkins' non-concrete works is just their resemblance to traditional forms. Atkins' way of contesting the mainstream was often to contest it within its own structures, so that his originality frequently resembles, in shape at least, the poetry that he attacks as insipid repetition of the past. The avant-garde techniques of so many Atkins poems are not a white imposition upon an essentially black language. They are a black American's remastery of the signifying materials of American English. They are a form of loud talk, wolfing, audacious reformation.

Works Cited

Atkins, Russell. "Henry Dumas: An Appreciation." *Black American Literature Forum* 22.2, 1988, pp. 159 – 60.

—, *Here in The*. Cleveland, OH: Cleveland State University Poetry Center, 1976.

—, *Heretofore*. London: Paul Breman, 1968.

—, "May Twenty-Second, Nineteen Sixty Seven." *Free Lance* 11.2, 1967: 20-23.

—, "Of." *Free Lance* 7.1, 1963: 21-23.

—, *A Podium Presentation*. Brooklyn Heights, OH: The Poetry Seminar Press, 1960.

—, "Review of Musophilus by Samuel Daniel." *Free Lance* 10.1, 1966: 12-13.

—, "Russell Atkins." *Contemporary Authors Autobiography Series*. Ed Joyce Nakamura. Vol. 16. Detroit: Gale Research Inc., 1992, pp. 1-19.

—, "Some Thoughts Defining 'Mainstream'…" *Free Lance* 8.1, 1964: 26-27.

Baraka, Amiri. *Home: Social Essays*. New York: William Morrow & Co., Inc., 1966.

Brooks, Gwendolyn. *Blacks*. Chicago: Third World Press, 1991.

Congdon, Kirby. "A Reply." *Input* 1.4, 1964: 9.

High, Ronald Henry. "Russell Atkins." *Dictionary of Literary Biography 41: Afro-American Poets since 1955*. Trudier Harris and Thadious Davis, eds. Detroit: Gale Research, 1985, pp. 24-32.

Hughes, Langston. "The Twenties: Harlem and its Negritude." *African Forum* 1, 1966: 18-19.

Johnson, Abby Arthur, and Ronald Mayberry Johnson. *Propaganda and Aesthetics: The Literary Politics of African-American Magazines in the Twentieth Century*. Amherst: University of Massachusetts Press, 1991.

Jordan, Casper LeRoy. "Afterword." *Phanomena.* Russell Atkins, pp. 76- 78.

Jordan, Casper LeRoy and J. Stefanski, eds. *Free Lance: Special Russell Atkins Issue* 14.2. 1970.

Moore, Marianne. Letter to Russell Atkins. 14 July 1951. Copy provided to the author by Russell Atkins.

Redmond, Eugene B. *Drumvoices: The Mission of Afro-American Poetry: A Critical History.* New York: Anchor/Doubleday, 1976.

Simon, Adelaide. "Salvos for Atkins." *Input* 1.4, 1964: 8-9.

Objects: For Russell Atkins

Aldon Lynn Nielsen

First Object

On June 1, 1964, Jim Lowell's Asphodel Bookshop published "The Cleveland Manifesto of Poetry." In keeping with the do it yourself aesthetic of the mid-century mimeo revolution, the manifesto was a single sheet, printed on both sides, subtitled "Principles behind the writings of 6 Cleveland Poets." The bookshop's announcement of their sponsorship of the manifesto is barely visible, appearing in reverse across the top of the first page. Readers used to the peculiarities of mimeo publishing might well at first have thought this credit line was simply bleeding through from page two, except that it is clearly not printed on page two. What object Lowell had in mind in posting publishing information in such a way that it could only be read in a mirror, if at all, is not recorded; perhaps he wanted to force readerly reflection, but in any event it seems to fit with the experimental thrust of the statements in poetics that he was issuing to a public. Despite the definite article in the manifesto's title, and the subtitle's implication of some modicum of unity in aesthetics, each of the six poets strikes a highly individual note. The statements are presented in no particular order, save that the two Russells, Russell Atkins and Russell Salamon, follow one another on the page.

Adelaide Simon, a colleague of Russell Atkins in the activities of the Free Lance workshop and journal, strikes the characteristically contrarian note:

> Get poetry off its knees and drop the post-Freudian Fuckisme, the Fake Religion (and/or Antireligion), the lapidary Greekery creakery crockery bit, and the weepily murderous introspection. Excuse me, Death is at the door, and my roses are burning.

Where Simon opens in full manifesto mode, Atkins starts with the most rhetorical of questions: "When the word 'poetry' is used as a noun to denote some recognizable thing on a page, is it also to be used to define poetry as a quality?" What Atkins is after is a way of thinking poetry *per se* beyond the more common appropriations of the term. He notes the "poetry" of the novel, "poetic" grammar, the poetry in science, but in the end he is left wondering if there can be a poetry of poetry. (Jayne Cortez seems to have answered in the affirmative in her poem of tribute to Aimé Césaire, which describes "A Certain Moment in History" when "his poetry became poetry unique to poetry" (93), a line that embodies Atkins' prescriptions for poetic redundance). If there can be a poetry of poetry, Atkins is certain it is not because some epiphanic leap of poetic insight has been condensed within the lines of the poem:

> One can scarcely think of classical poets who depended upon "insight" per se, for "poetry". The chance that "insight" will be anything at all is one in a thousand. That it will be revelatory is one in a million. . . . *If there is scientific science; if there is dramatic*

drama; if there is "musical" music; perhaps there is "poetic" poetry.

Though, to judge from Adelaide Simon's list of don'ts for contemporary poets, there may be precious little of the latter in evidence.

Atkins reproduced his portion of the Cleveland manifesto just a few months later in the special Cleveland issue of *Input*, where he added a note on the history of the Free Lance Workshop. The importance of Lowell's Asphodel Bookshop to the group can be judged from Atkins' comments on the isolation he had felt in Cleveland, a place where, according to him, "lecturing celebrities of the literary world seemed to come . . . as one might have gone to Anchorage," and where "bookstores [knew] nothing of Beloit, Experiment, Trace etc. They knew only the dignity of the hardback book where the poet and even the novelist were concerned: very square hardbacks" (6). Atkins claims that *Free Lance* was rare among little mags in that, with its publication of his psychovisualism essays, it had advanced a "complete and original . . . bid for a 'scientific aesthetic'" (7). While the journal had published many of the Beats, and had taken the early work of Robert Creeley and Irving Layton, *Free Lance*, according to Atkins, "did not advocate the Carlos Williams school . . . It never held any particular sympathy for that concern with 'ordinary language'" (7).

In writing of Clarence Major, a poet Russell Atkins published in *Free Lance*, Keith Byerman has remarked that "His goal is a new thing, a new object in the world to be understood the way we understand other objects, including ourselves; at the same time, he wants to suggest the inherent mystery, the ultimate unknowability that is part of the world and part of such a text" (Byerman 115). In this Major was in full agreement with Atkins, who in many places has recorded his sense that a poem or a piece of music is, every bit as much as is a sculpture or painting, an object in the world. William Carlos Williams had long stressed the *thingness* of the poem, and while Atkins was so much at odds with others of Williams's imperatives, he was with him on this score. The Human phenomenon, Atkins was to insist, "is an object-forming animal" (*Juxtapositions* 1). Few would argue with this much of Atkins' sense of the human being as *Homo faber.* And yet, however many would see Atkins as clearly being in league with Jorge Luis Borges's sense of the poet as *el hacedor,* there could not have been many among Atkins' contemporaries who, as he did, considered the object-forming process as "the basis of technique" (*Juxtapositions* 1) in their works. Atkins speaks of the "possible right a thing has to be brought into existence":

> Thus, when a poem, or idea, or "musical" work occurs to me, I don't question whether it will be relevant or whether it will communicate or "mean," I simply indulge its drive to *be* brought into existence, its drive to be. Creativity for creativity's sake: This may be confused with "art for art's sake." They are not the same, but may complement one another. (*Juxtapositions* 2)

In much of this, Atkins may be seen as clearly in the tradition of Williams ("no ideas but in things") and the Objectivist poets who followed in the Thirties. Yet he just as clearly parts company with them, and with the critical traditions leading up to them, in the techniques that he derives from this similar starting point. Atkins declares that his work:

> Indulges in its own principles without the slightest intention of conforming to contemporary poetic shibboleths, such as "understatement," "economy," "precision," Ruskin's "presentability," and, for the poetry-dramas, no encouragement of Blackmur's "mea-

> sured prose." Instead, in the dramas, poetry is based on *orchestral poetics*, i.e., "Musical" devices: 1) it is scored like a ton of bricks, using words for maximum momentum, volume, and *"doubling" by manipulating the implicit in a set of grammatical categories* as, e.g., a single melody upon two different sounding instruments. (*Juxtapositions* 3)

So, where he follows the Objectivist poets in their dedication to thinking with the things of this world along a line of melody, and while he shares their view of clarity as a matter of objective vision rather than transparency of verbal constructions, he rejects their post-Imagist drive for economies of expression, and takes a positive relish in redundancy. As he argues in a "Manifesto" of his own later, "If a thing is good enough to be said once, it is good enough to be repeated in some form immediately and thereafter" (*Juxtapositions* 10), because for Atkins the important thing is the manifestation of the created object as, to use his expression, "*stimuli extension*."

That individual manifesto, reprinted in Atkins' 1991 retrospective chapbook *Juxtapositions*, is a fifteen point unfolding of the implications of his contribution to "The Cleveland Manifesto of Poetry." At the outset, Atkins underscores his insistence on art as a bringing-into-existence. Here, too, he follows Williams, who insisted that art is not to mirror nature, but rather to do as nature does, to bring the new into existence. But, contra Williams, Atkins also insists that "Art should encourage mannerism," and it is in this unusual admixture of modernist objectivity and neobaroque dedication to conspicuous technique, to adopt another of Atkins' terms, that we see just how out of step with many of his contemporaries he was. Atkins' manifesto urges poets to avoid the destruction of the poem in the interests of clarity. He holds that all vocal registers should be acceptable, and that the artist should be self-indulgent, as the artist is the "source of everything," (9) solipsism be damned. Directly contesting the advice given to writers of both poetry and non-fiction ever since the Pound era, Atkins advises that the poet should distract the reader. This is not meant in the sense of offering a distraction from the weight of everyday life, nor is it like the magician distracting his audience so that he can sneak the elephant onto the stage. Rather, Atkins wants the reader distracted from that which readers are intent upon doing, sense-making. "Generally, the casual reader goes straight for the 'sense' or the 'meaning' behind the words (as some alcoholics want to get full" (10). Atkins holds that there is nothing lodged "behind" the words, and that the words themselves are to be seen as performative, a view too often left out of account in critiques of "performance poetry" to this day. As he had rejected Williams's advocacy of ordinary language, Atkins eschews the Yeatsian imperative to seek the natural words in their natural order. "If possible," he insists, the poet should "avoid saying anything in poetry as it would ordinarily be said." He wants a language of poetry like that Cortez credits to Césaire, "a language 'peculiar' to itself" (11). This seemingly verges on the structuralists' never-fulfilled dream of locating features unique to "literary language." (Free indirect discourse had a habit of turning up in the common speech of ordinary speaking subjects, as did nearly every other feature proposed by the projects of structuralism as possibly forming a binary opposition between literary and non-literary.) But what Atkins is after is an entirely aesthetic use of language, one that may succeed no better than the structuralists in establishing its uniqueness, but which certainly set him apart from the mainstream of North American poetry in the twentieth century and beyond. "*Art* does not have to *convince*" (11), and therefore it does not have to "work" in the sense usually enforced in writing workshops. Poetry does not have to communicate with an audience. "It is a phenomenalism" (12). In the end, Atkins cautions against the desire to "write the 'good' or the 'best' of anything." "Art does not have to 'work'," he insists. "It *is*" (16). For all that this position echoes MacLeish's "*Ars Poetica*," it is important to note that Atkins' manifestoes take the same manifest delight in their own impossibility as does the MacLeish poem. MacLeish prescribes a mute and palpable poem, though in those very lines he propounds a simile. Atkins argues against being bound to the sense-hunting instincts of the poetry audience, knowing full well that any object made of words is immediately subject to acts of interpretation. Baraka's landmark "Black Art," published just a few years after the Cleveland Poets' manifesto, is a lyric manifesto that calls for a poem to be, lemons piled on a stoop, resembling nothing so much as the globed fruit of MacLeish's first stanza. Few poets could be more different from one another than Archibald MacLeish, Amiri Baraka and Russell Atkins, and yet each has derived from the modernist revolution a sense of the verbal construct as an object form.

Such an aesthetic position would seemingly place Atkins at odds with the Black Aesthetic Movement that arose midway through his career. There is no doubt that Atkins had many disagreements with individual propositions advanced by advocates of the Black Arts in the sixties and early seventies, but none of that was an obstacle to his playing a role in the movement. He, along with Norman Jordan, was instrumental in the founding of Cleveland's Muntu Poets group, whose activities were noted in the pages of *Black World* magazine. The group took its name from the same Bantu vocabulary from which Paul Carter-Harrison derived the title of his collection of Black plays, *Kuntu Drama,* and, like Carter-Harrison, the Cleveland group had read of this Bantu linguistic philosophy in the pages of Jahnheinz Jahn's *Muntu: An Outline of New African*

Culture, a book that was widely influential in the United States following the 1961 publication of the English language edition. Adelaide Simon had noted in her own contribution to the *Input* Cleveland issue that Atkins had been in correspondence with Jahn, who stopped by Cleveland to visit the poet. With this history before us, it is easier to see that Atkins' experimentalism was not a matter simply of modernist influence, for the modernists had already passed through Africa on their way to Atkins. As critics and poets from Alain Locke to C.L.R. James to Melvin B. Tolson had long established, modernist form was itself derived in large part from prior African modalities. Jahn's *Muntu* posited a modern, neo-African diasporic culture, and the neo-Baroque of so much New World culture was traceable to African sources. The objectivism of modernity was, for a Russell Atkins, a mode of intellectual homecoming. More important, in revisiting the Black Arts Movement we see increasingly how capacious it truly was, and how scholars may have been too quick to see an opposition between Atkins' insistence upon the performative values of inscription and the purported privileging of the oral among Black Arts poets. Amiri Baraka is quick to remind students of black writing that : "The Oral Tradition, so called, is too often the sleekest form of socio-aesthetic 'Dis' going around. That is, to harp on the Black Oral Tradition sometimes is a *screen* for distorting the fact that African cultures were also the first to commit the oralture to artifact" (256).

Juxtapositions reproduces a Q & A titled "The Following: Misconceptions Relating to My Poetry-Drama, Poems-in-Play-Form, etc. (Subtitle: Somewhat silly comments made by others as 'critics')," though one suspects both sides of the interview are Atkins. In closing that Q & A, Atkins argues straight-forwardly enough that our decision as to whether or not something "works" is conditioned by our expectations of what that thing is to accomplish. On his view, such audience expectations are not something with which artists should concern themselves. His aesthetic is more ontological. *Is* the work what the artist wants it to *be*? The question is never, "does the poem convey the artist's intention?" It is instead a matter of the artist's intending to put a new object into the world. And to that end, Atkins published, among so many other things, three chapbooks titled *Objects*.

Objects

Three years before contributing to the Cleveland Poets' manifesto, Atkins had published the first of his *Objects* chapbooks with the Eureka, California, avant garde small press, Hearse, in an edition of two hundred copies. The first poem in the collection is an instance of much that Atkins was to advocate in his aesthetic prescriptions. Titled "Objects on a Table," the poem doesn't appear to offer up recognizable descriptions of any familiar objects, on a table or elsewhere. It is somewhat reminiscent of poem number 1 (which is not the first poem) in George Oppen's first volume, *Discrete Series*: "white. From the / Under arm of T" (Oppen 3). Oppen's poem, published by the Objectivist Press nearly three decades before Atkins' chapbook, reads like a riddle poem, if we approach it with the expectation that it is describing something. Word is that Oppen was looking at an elevator, though the lines could as easily be describing an old time traffic signal, as I on first reading supposed they did. The poem's third, and longest, stanza gives us:

> Up
> Down. Round
> Shiny fixed
> Alternatives

Objects
Russell
Atkins

These are alternative directions, alternative prospective movements, alternatives to, or seen from, the ground. The punctuation and enjambment work in conjunction with the visual structure of the poem. "Up Down" is a sentence given to us by a period, an inaudible full stop. "Up" is above "down" on the page. They stand as alternatives, yet they are fixed alternatives.

In his notes to the poem, Michael Davidson quotes a 1963 Oppen letter in which the poet describes the particular device found over elevator doors at the time of composition as "so familiar at the time" that he didn't think "anyone was puzzled at the time" (359), to which we might well reply, anyone who already knew there was an elevator involved. Of far greater import is the poem's allusion to the "limited alternatives of a culture" represented , but, and here is the key relationship to Atkins, the real importance, as Williams was to remark in his review of Oppen's book, "cannot be in what the poem says." That, according to Williams, would be a redundancy (though, as we've seen, Atkins did not share Williams's aversion to the redundant). No, "the importance lies in what the poem is" (qtd. In Davidson, 358).

We encounter a similarly riddling verbal landscape at the outset of the first poem in Atkins' book: "It is flat's streak that attacks / the hollow of lapse" (n.pag.) Here it is the poem's title that plays to the casual reader's interpretive zeal. Where Oppen just calls his poem "1," Atkins gives the reader a title that arouses assumptions that an act of description is at hand. "Flat's streak" might encourage us to think we are reading a description of something to do with flatware, or with a streak on the flat surface of the table. But of greater import is the construction of sound forms in these lines: "flat's," "attacks," "lapse." The characteristic syntactic attack of Atkins soon makes clear enough that, no matter the poem's point of origin, the words' possible links to objects outside the poem are not really the point. Can we be sure that the apostrophe in "flat's" is denoting possession? Any who had read other Atkins poems before coming to this book would be familiar with his trademark deployment of the apostrophe for visual as well as syntactic effect. The sibilance of these seemingly sibyllic lines has as much material presence as any objects outside the poem.

The poem's second stanza distributes vowel sounds to much the same end:

> Of alarm like takes you
> and finally, a whirl to slur
> Whereto?

The rhyming of "you" and "whereto" following "attacks" and "lapse" in the preceding couplet, makes for an anticipation of further line-end resonance, but, as in Williams's wheelbarrow poem, what Atkins is after is more a seeding of repeated tones throughout the lines. And so we get "half," "Janet," "fact," "ash," and "distances" spread through the poem to ring off the opening stanza's "attacks" and "lapse." We hear "dusk," "up," "crumbles," "once" and "flung" to form chordal patterns with "you" and "whereto," and so on. These effects produce a coherent sound object that is the poem.

But just as with the work of the earlier Objectivists, anything made of words retains an attachment to the world of sense, just as much as it appeals to the senses. The rhetorical question "Whereto?" will, no matter Atkins' aversion to talk of what works in poetry, continue to work at the reader's mind. That, though, is just as much a part of Atkins' intentions as are these sound structures. For even as Atkins wants a poem that has a certain visual structure on the page, and a sound structure in our hearing, his theory of psychovisualism holds that the object form of the poem is a structure within the mind, as much as it has existence anywhere. "Object form" had a grammatical meaning long before Atkins adopted the term, think of the object forms of the personal pronoun, and since his writing the term has come to be used in the information technology field. There has always been something of the Platonic about the idea, though conjoining "object" to "form" would appear to manifest a logical problem if we were restricting ourselves to the Platonic field. In a sense, the Atkins object-form dissolves the traditional view of the form/content opposition. For Atkins, there is no separable content. The poem is an object form presented for our attention. When we come to the poem's declaration that "Over the way is half Janet," we can easily enough make "sense" of the line in relationship to the following line's reference to dusk, and we would most likely conjure a Janet half in shadow. The full stanza, though, makes it hard to hold to such a sensible reading:

> Over the way is half Janet
> Nearby, dusk-struck
> trembling of up
> in fact

The sense-making strain in my makeup hears an echo of "color-struck" in "dusk-struck," but is that because I know that I am reading an African American poet, or simply because the terms make a mode of rhyme in my memory? Can I hear "dumb struck" as well? Is the nearness of half Janet causing the nearby trembling? And what can it mean that it is "up" that is doing the trembling? This does not seem to be the antirationalism of much modernist experiment. It runs against the tide of imagism, and yet there is little doubt that the poem conjures images. At the poem's close, "everything's hopelessly white / and flung" – flung with "everything" (as if a magician had suddenly yanked away the white table cloth leaving everything else trembling on the table's surface) is our usual way of reading for meaning. Again, it's not that Atkins expects that we can suppress our zeal for interpretation, nor that we can be supposed to appreciate the poem purely as sound, but the sound/meaning structures formed in our reading continue to hover, trembling in their ultimate undecideability. In mathematics, an undecidable problem is one that no algorithm can solve. That does not mean it is not a problem. In computability theory, the term has a somewhat different meaning, and the fact that there are competing meanings of "undecidability" is an instance of what we have learned from poststructuralism, that undecidability is a condition of possibility for interpretation. Atkins, despite being an early proponent of one sort of deconstruction, was no post-structuralist, but in his life's work he had worked his way into many of the same issues. It is not that a poem such as the one that opens Objects cannot be read, or cannot mean, but that it cannot be unread and cannot stop meaning. It is a "trembling of up / in fact." This "up," like Oppen's, remains an alternative, but this time a trembling alternative.

Atkins' first *Objects* includes many of the poems that have come to be most often reprinted and discussed, to the extent that any of Atkins' work has been collected and discussed. "It's Here in The," the poem that gave its title to the Cleveland State University Press selection of the poets' work, is here, along with "Furious'd Garb," "Trainyard at Night," "Night and a Distant Church" and "Narrative." Each is, as MacLeish would have had it, a palpable thing in the world. Each is a performance. And a few of them reappear in Objects 2, though appearing differently.

Objects 2

Objects was followed two years later by the chapbook *Objects 2,* published by Cleveland's Renegade Press. This was the small press run by poet d.a. levy, who had been supported and encouraged by members of the Free Lance group from the outset. Following an early version of "couch surfing," levy had bunked in the basements of multiple Free Lancers, and he operated Renegade Press from the basement of Adelaide Simon, who had taken him under her wing. The last page of *Objects 2* bears a note advertising other publications from Renegade, but also calling attention to *Free Lance.*

We can get a strong sense of Atkins' experiences trying to get his work out into the world from two very different responses he had gotten from his elders in the poetry world. In 1950, Arna Bontemps wrote to Atkins from his desk at the Fisk University library, reacting to poems that the Cleveland poet had sent him:

> Typographical poetry is not my idiom, but I have examined with interest your compositions in that form. We'll just have to wait and see what the future holds for this type of expression, but I'm pretty sure that most of the publishers we know are not ready for it.

In contrast, Marianne Moore wrote to Atkins just eight months later requesting that he send her copies of two of his more experimental poems in time for a July 13 broadcast of *The World in Books* on WEVD radio. She writes to Atkins again following the broadcast to apologize for not reciting the poem live as well as she had done in rehearsal, but assures Atkins that none-the-less, what she in her earlier letter had called his "locomotive poem" had been the hit of the program. In that follow-up letter she identifies the poem

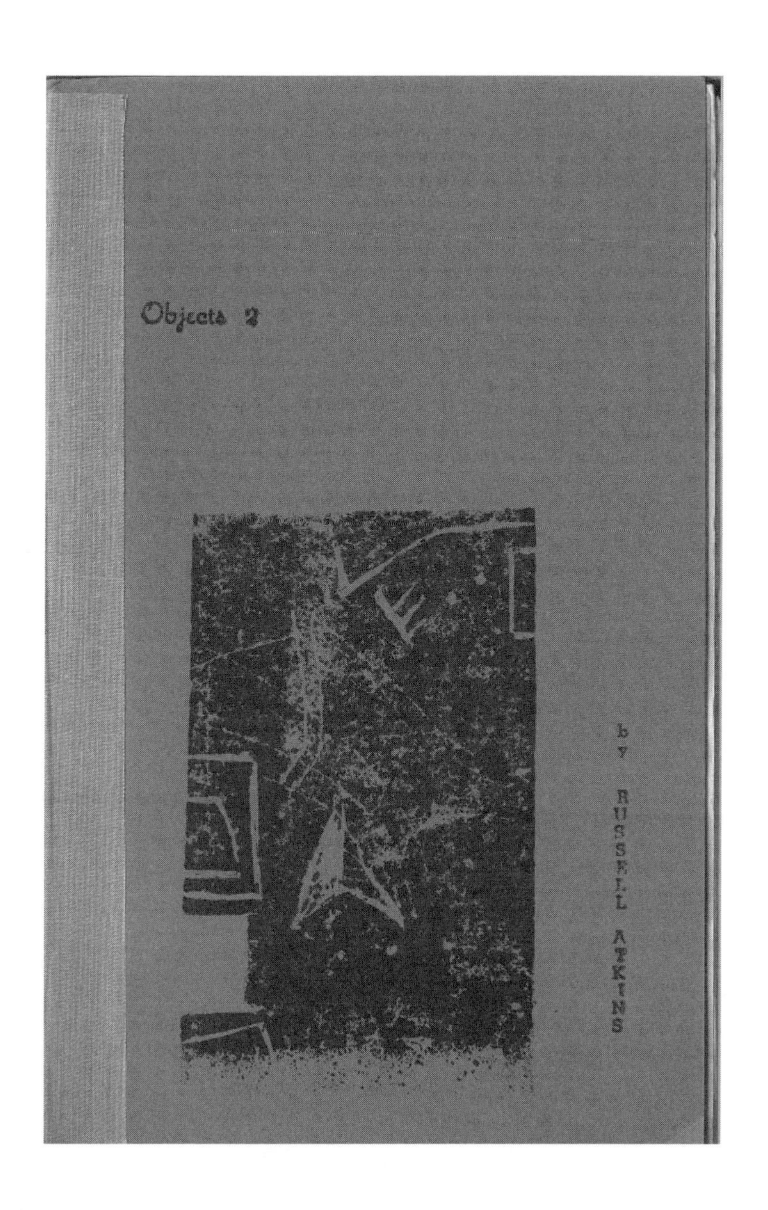
Objects 2
by RUSSELL ATKINS

by its title, "Trainyard by Night," and that is the title as it appears in the 1963 *Objects 2,* though a manifestly different form of the poem had appeared in the first *Objects*, a bit closer in time to Moore's correspondence, with a different preposition in its title. It was then published as "Trainyard at Night."

"At" or "by;" "at" may be a function word used to indicate a position in time, whereas "by" has the sense of "during the course of." "Trainyard at Night," presumably the form of the poem read over the radio by Moore, or at least having the form of the poem's title, makes use of typographical scoring from the outset:

> ThandUNandDER TH and UN and DER
>   TH   UN   UN
>   andDER   DER
>
> (*Objects*)

We do not know just how Moore intoned this passage; perhaps she gave greater vocal emphasis to the capitalized letters. But there is a further effect available in the visual form of the poem, which brings the word "under' out from under the vocables, as if a sort of underwriting insured the structure. Both versions of the poem, like the poem "Narrative," close in sound effects, in this instance miming the sound of the locomotive:

> . . . insisting on hissing hiss
> hiss s ss ss sss s
> sss   s s
> s

"Trainyard by Night," the poem as it appears in *Objects 2*, is not underscored in quite the same manner, and yet it has its own visual scoring. The first line of the poem here reads simply "A THUNDER," with the words all in caps.

Except that there was at least one printing of the chapbook in which these two words appear in a different, archaic font. It is quite possible that levy, who did the printing by hand, was having a bit of fun, but in any event what we are left with is a set of differing objects, forming around Atkins' original set of conceptions. "Trainyard at Night" moves from thc thunderous typography to a line that reads, "its huge big bold blasts black." The "same" line in "Trainyard by Night" reads, "then huge bold blasts bluff." Both forms give us an alliterative line with natural pauses between the words, so that even though the line makes use of none of the typographic techniques that gave Bontemps pause, each still causes anyone reading the poem aloud to slow down and enunciate in short bursts, rather like the bursts of locomotive steam at the close of the poem. As much as the poem's persona describes himself as listening to the approach of "the great Limited," the poem is not so much a reproduction of real sounds in the natural world as it is the construction of forms taking their impetus from that real world. These are not signs taking the place of the train, they are things placed in the same world as the train.

Changes in other poems are smaller, and could even be typesetting errors, but there they are. "Night and a Distant Church," for instance, reads in its second line, "the mmm mm," but the version in *Objects 2* has the line as "then mmm mm," quite a different matter at the level of semantics. Both versions close with characteristic Atkins concrete playfulness:

ells
b

ells
b

Many will see (hear?) "hell's bells" emerging from the distant church, but this disjunctive typography also gives us "ells" that "b" ("ells be"), an "ell" being something L-shaped, but also a unit of measurement, rounding out Atkins' measures.

No doubt this sort of thing would have greatly interested the Marianne Moore who so often altered her own poems following their initial publication, had she known of such transformations. It may be hard for us to get at Atkins' object in these changes, but the more important thing is to register their difference, to behold in them not simply differing instantiations of a "same" poem, but to see them as distinct objects in a field of poetry. When *reading* Atkins, a poet who held that music sang to a visual apparatus in our minds, we should never lose sight of the object-form as inextricable sound/sight phenomenon.

Objects for Piano

Which may in its turn help us to see what Atkins is up to with the third and final entry in the *Objects* chapbooks series, *Objects for Piano*. Published in 1969, this is the only one of the three to appear under the Free Lance Press imprint. The work is dedicated to the memory of Adelaide Simon, colleague in the arts to Russell Atkins, host to d.a. levy, and community activist in Cleveland. One of Simon's poetic works, "Permit Me Voyage," had an accompanying drawing produced by levy. *Objects for Piano* is identified as a "collection," so we may read its four sections as a discrete series, related compositional objects.

This music was first performed in public by pianist Dolores White. In a recent email comment, White, who checked her memory with Simon's husband, the cellist Martin Simon, reports:

russell
atkins
Objects
for PIANO

> Russell Atkins is a friend of mine that I respect very much. He is a unique and special person. His music in my opinion expands the boundaries of music as we know it. He sets his own standards and language of music composition. It is unconventional in style, interested in a wide variety of musical genres, poetic design: he invents his own system/uncommon creativity and his music is delivered with a palpable, infectious joy. It is engaging.

This is no doubt an apt way to speak of a composition that opens with two lines in two-four time, both in the subbass clef, maybe. The clef signs are missing their dots. That first piece then shifts into 3/4 time and passes through sections in 5/8 and 6/8 before ending. These time shifts are characteristic of the piece, as we can see in this reproduction of a page from part 2:

A note informs us that the first section was composed in 1954, though none of the remaining sections is dated.

We know that the work was completed by 1963, as that was the year in which the performance took place, the same year in which *Objects 2* was published. It is possible that the work underwent further changes in the six years between first performance and publication of the chapbook. Another feature of *Objects for Piano* worthy of note is that it is the only one of the three that reproduces Atkins' original inscription. The entire piece is scored by hand, and a comparison with another of Atkins' scores, "Object Forms," confirms that this is the poet's own hand.

Session musicians often speak of their dread of "the black page," the page of a composition suddenly thrust before them that presents difficulties they are expected to surmount; "The black page" because of the sheer number of notes on the score. *Objects for Piano* is not as densely printed as the score, for example, of Frank Zappa's "The Black Page," but it presents challenges from its opening direction ("AGITATED") to its final rest. It is, to harken back to the composer's comments in *Juxtapositions*, "scored like a ton of bricks." It is most certainly a piece to be played, though it has seldom been played, but it is just as much an object to be looked at. Recent years have seen a small movement to resuscitate the traditions of sheet music, not so much for the concert hall, where it has never gone away, but for home use, as in the days before record players when people collected and played sheet music at home. *Objects for Piano* represents something a bit different, perhaps closer to Celia Zukofsky's contributions to her husband's works. It is a music chap book, inserted into the world of small press publishing as something to be collected, read, looked over. The key may be on the cover. The uncredited figure drawn on the front of *Objects for Piano* is a partial reproduction of one of the figures from Atkins' "A Psychovisual Manual for Compositional Deconstruction and Sound Applied," published in *Free Lance* in the previous decade. That figure, not explained in the chapbook, was developed by Atkins as a way of illustrating his method for determining the number of measures a musical figure should occupy, but, in its resemblance to the ocular mechanism, it also serves as a sign of Atkins' commitment to the idea that music composition depends upon, not the retina, but the visual mechanism to achieve compositional shape. Which is as much as to say that a musical composition is as much a verbal composition as it is an object form placed in the world.

It was another composer, a black composer, Hale Smith, who set one of Atkins' object forms to music. Smith's 1953 composition "In Memoriam – Beryl Rubinstein" includes texts by Langston Hughes and Russell Atkins in a tribute to the late director of the Cleveland Institute of Music, someone Smith, Atkins and the Simons had all known and worked with. A recording was produced by the Cleveland Composers' Guild, featuring Robert Shaw conducting the Kulas Choir and Chamber Orchestra. As the piece comes to its end, we hear the choir softly making its way through a field of prepositions, watching, along with the poem's persona, as a keening light:

> over the crucial earth
> is up
> and dying over

The sun is certainly a shiny alternative, however unfixed. But in Atkins' words, trembling in the chorus, we are both up and over, as in over head, above; as in over, at an end.

Works Cited

Atkins, Russell. "Russell Atkins." *Input* 1.4 (1964) 6-7. Print.

—. *Juxtapositions*. N.p: Cleveland, OH: 1991. print.

—. *Objects*. Eureka, CA: Hearse Press, 1961. N. pag. Print.

—. *Objects 2*. Cleveland, OH: Renegadc Press, 1963. N. Pag. Print.

—. *Objects for Piano*. Cleveland, OH: The Free Lance Press, 1969. Print.

Atkins, Russell, and Russell Salamon, Adelaide Simon, Jau Billera, d.a. levy and Kent Taylor. "The Cleveland Manifesto of Poetry." Cleveland, OH : The Asphodel Bookshop, 1964. Print.

Baraka, Amiri. "Black Poetry & the Oral Tradition." *Razor: Revolutionary Art for Cultural Revolution*. Chicago: Third World Press, 2012. 256-63. Print.

Bontemps, Arna. Lettr to Russell Atkins. 9 November 1950. Copy in possession of author.

Byerman, Keith. *The Art and Life of Clarence Major*. Athens, GA: U of Georgia P, 2012. Print.

Cortez, Jayne. *somewhere in advance of nowhere*. New York: Serpent's Tail Press, 1996. Print.

Davidson, Michael. "Notes." *George Oppen: New and Collected Poems*. Ed. Michael Davidson. New York: New Directions P, 2002. Print.

Moore, Marianne. Letter to Russell Atkins. 7 July 1951. Copy in possession of author.

—. Letter to Russell Atkins of 19 July 1951. Copy in possession of author.

Oppen, George. *Collected Poems*. New York: New Directions, 1975. Print.

Smith, Hale. "In Memoriam." *Music of Hale Smith*. Composers Recordings CRI. B00004WJMO. 2000.

White, Dolores. Email to the author. 26 July 2012.

"To Be Set To Music":
The Rhetorical-Aural Poetry-Dramas of Russell Atkins

Tyrone Williams

Russell Atkins is one of the most significant literary innovators within the African Diaspora tradition as manifest in the United States of America during the first three quarters of the 20th century. Although there are strands of affiliation between Atkins' deconstruction of received literary forms and the revisionist strategies of other African American innovators in poetry (e.g., Melvin B. Tolson, Nathaniel Mackey, Fred Moten and Harryette Mullen come to mind), Atkins' reconstruction of received anachronistic forms remains unique. Aside from the dazzling virtuosity displayed by his psycho-visual poems, the rhetorical-aural effects of what he calls poetry-dramas underscore Atkins' debt to European opera and Elizabethan rhetoric on the one hand and the American Gothic tradition on the other hand.[1] Most significant, these traditions abut American Midwestern speech patterns and dialect forms. The result of these "juxtapositions" (as he titles his 1991 collection of critical essays, aesthetic manifestos and poems) is a series of volatile, and often violent, rhetorical and dramatic effects. Finally, Atkins' interest in experimental music and training as an avant-garde musician might explain why these poetry-dramas were all—with one important exception—subtitled "To Be Set To Music." Although there is anecdotal evidence that Atkins did indeed compose and record the music for these pieces,[2] which we may regard as librettos, I am interested here in the semantic implications of the subtitles in relation to these syntactically staged rhetorical effects and the resulting aesthetic, social and cultural gestures toward violence.

Atkins has been candid about his interest in the aesthetic violence occasioned by his various modes of rhetorical miscegenation.[3] Aesthetic violence opens the path to the new; as such, Atkins' use of violence may be understood as the logical consequence of a valorization of innovation per se. In the context of the poetry-dramas' subtitles, innovation is linked to both present-day rhetorical-literary effects (e.g., the shattering of traditional genres) and future rhetorical-musical effects (which, in this context, remain speculative). That is, the poetry-dramas as published are merely one mode of creative experimentation (rhetorical); the subtitles point to future experiments in rhetorical-musical genres.

This apotheosis of experimentation links Atkins to a certain strain within modernism and New Criticism even though Atkins is explicit in his denunciation of another strain within these aesthetic and critical movements, that which emphasizes taste ("moderation"), understood as syntactical and semantic symmetry (what Atkins disparages as "balance" and "ambiguity").[4] At the same time Atkins' interest in the American Gothic tradition and its emphasis on effect suggests a correspondence with Edgar Allan Poe's "Philosophy on Composition." In this well-known essay the short story writer and poet notes his preference for "... commencing with the consideration of an effect." Poe is interested in the production of effect as an underutilized aesthetic within the parameters of art, e.g., the sublime.

Atkins, on the other hand, asserts no interest in art per se, though he has "nothing against art for art's sake." (Preface) Instead, Atkins advocates "Creativity for creativity's sake!" We may regard this statement as a gesture toward the possible, given what Atkins says about his own creativity. Noting that the "human phenomenon" is "an object-forming animal," not unlike "birds, spiders, beavers, etc.," his "works are to be regarded as [his] own object-forming processes at work and amount to an objectification of mental life taking the forms of books, manuscripts, notated music." (Preface) Objectification is, here, a reduction of possibility; apparently, Atkins' "mental life" can only create art, and thus, he validates, per Poe, the aesthetic above all else: "13) ART: Art does not have to *convince*. Its aim is largely AESTHETIC, not essentially informative or 'problem solving,' or trying to 'tell anyone anything.' THEREFORE: 'beauty,' being its own value, is to be defined ONLY by the artist as he immerses himself in the bringing-into-existence-as-creativity process. Nothing the artist does is *obligated* to 'work' for or 'communicate' with an audience. It is a phenomenalist about which the audience is *relatively* free." ("Manifesto") The apparent contradiction or, at least, tension between "Creativity" and "Art" may be understood as analogous to the Platonic distinction between Forms and forms, Ideals and things. Aristotle would, of course, reverse the Platonic hierarchy in order to find a place for poetry and drama within the Republic, that is, within human society and history. Atkins' remarks in his "Preface" follow suit: "I function on the premise of the possible right a thing has to be brought into existence...I simply indulge its drive to be brought into existence, its drive to be." The "possible right" of the "thing" is, as a conditional, analogous to a future "to be." Though that future is dependent on a conscious "I" in order "to be brought into existence," dependency neutralizes neither its "drive" nor its "right" to exist. The reorientation of the ego from ends to means of creativity, the imputation of an ethos, if not animus, to the thing, follows the "early" New Critical and modernist elevation of the art work over and above its creator.[5] At the same time some of Atkins' pronouncements in *Juxtapositions* and elsewhere follow contrary strains in New "early" Criticism and modernism that elevate the creator over his or her creation (e.g., Joyce). Despite his rejection of second-generation New Critical values—"understatement," "economy," "precision,"...and "Blackmur's 'measured prose'"—Atkins, like later innovators who would also embrace decidedly anti-humanist poetics (e.g., Language Writing, Oulipo, chance operations, etc.), endorses, however unwittingly, some of its first-generation tenets. (Preface) For example, while Joel Spingarn, who rejected the relevance of moral or ethical considerations regarding either the creation or interpretation of art objects, may be regarded as a fellow traveler, Poe, whose "Philosophy of Composition" may be read as a precursor of "criticism" as it developed throughout the 19th century in the United States, is his philosophical and literary ancestor.

This particular validation of "early" New Critical tenets was published in 1991 but similar ideas can be found in other works throughout Atkins' career. However, as much as these statements would seem to support Poe's views as expressed in his "Philosophy of Composition," a caveat is essential: the last sentence of section thirteen from "Manifesto" makes it clear that Atkins is interested, here, in the freedom of both the artist and the audience.[6] In the context of African American life in Cleveland in the first half of the 20th century such a stance, however misunderstood, was a call to artists to reject African American "culture" to the extent it was largely, if not only, a by-product of slavery and racism. Over and above a culture conceived as narrowcasting a predetermined set of cultural, social and political norms, Atkins imagines his art as broadcasting innovations, an opening up of the aesthetic field within the larger domain of African American culture and life. Given the significance of African American innovations in music, however stereotyped, vis-à-vis American culture, we may thus understand "to be set to music" as both a reimagining of the future possibilities of all American music and, more particularly, a re-envisioning of what counts—and doesn't count—as African-American music and, more generally, African American culture.[7] As evidence for this claim, I want to examine a few of Atkins poetry-dramas within the purview of "conspicuous technique," a phrase he first uses in an essay in *Juxtapositions.* Discussing the poetry-dramas separately from the poetry is not unproblematic since many of the original books and chapbooks Atkins published were conceived as whole art works or creative opuses. Consequently my excision of the poetry-dramas from their original contexts, however pragmatic and, indeed, New Critical, must qualify the following analyses.[8]

If we regard conspicuous technique as a set of experiments in rhetorical violence, we might be surprised that one of Atkins' earliest attempts at a poetry-drama, "The Nail," written in 1957 but not published until 1970, reads as an example of moderate—not conspicuous—technique. The project, which was suggested to Atkins, is his adaptation of a short story by the 19th c. Spanish writer Pedero Antonio Alarcon. *Contra* Poe's insistence on condensed narration for maximum effect, "The Nail" is one of Atkins' longest works. The protagonist is a widow, Gabriela Zahara, who, at the beginning of the play, has been traveling under an assumed name, Blanca. She meets Felipe, a gentleman, at an inn while awaiting her coach. He is immediately enthralled by her but she puts him off; she is, she says, "dead" to love. Felipe is on his way to see his good friend, Zarco, who has recently been appointed a judge. Felipe tells him he met a bewitching woman on the train but Zarco has lost his interest in love since his betrothed, Mercedes, abandoned him. Having lost faith in love, Zarco is consumed with the "law" and relates to Felipe the case of a missing wife whose husband, dead for two years, has been reexamined (during an exhumation) and found to have been murdered by a nail to the head. Consumed by his distrust of women, of love, Zarco spins out a narrative that indicts the missing wife for cold-hearted murder though, as Felipe reminds him, his narrative has no basis in actual fact. Zarco decrees that a *judicium in absentia*, a trial of the missing murderer, be held. Shortly thereafter, Mercedes, Zarco's missing betrothed, shows up to explain that she had to leave him because she was married, however unhappily. Before she can explain more, Felipe re-enters and is stunned to see Mercedes, and she, him, for she is also "his" Blanca. As one might expect in this melodrama, Mercedes, *aka*/Blanca, is also Gabriela Zahara; she interrupts her own trial in absentia in order to explain why she murdered her husband (he was abusive). Zarco is stunned to discover that "his" Mercedes is Zahara, but still signs the death certificate, albeit in a daze. After discovering from Felipe that Gabriela still loves him, Zarco tries to issue a stay of execution. The end of the play is deliberately ambiguous. After "the murderer" is executed, Felipe sees her closed coffin and weeps, assuming it is Gabriela's, but at the end of the play, Zarco, renouncing his allegiance to the law, runs off with a "woman," who looks like one "dead." in a late-night coach.

"The Nail" lacks the characteristic rhetorical devices, and thus the conspicuous techniques, that would come to define Atkins' other poetry-dramas. Instead, this adaptation relies on Poe's macabre affectations, Shakespeare's array of pseudonyms and disguises, and the predominant themes of German and Italian opera: death and love. As in Poe, a ghoulish, if "offstage," death orients the narrative of "The

Nail." And as in Shakespeare, multiple identities ensure duplicity: Gabriela deceives Zarco as Mercedes and Felipe as Blanca. Even death is both doubled and duplicitous: Gabriela killed because she was "killed" by a husband whose public charms turned out to be a cover for private cruelty. However, what makes "The Nail" more than just a mash-up of Poe, Shakespeare and operatic melodrama is its explicit critique of the law of the proper name insofar as it facilitates social and cultural conformity. Gabriela's pseudonyms facilitate her flight from matrimony and Zarco's judgment (in the Kantian sense) to flee with the woman in the coach overrides the legalism of his judgeship. Both abandon their social and cultural roles. Thus "The Nail" announces almost all the themes Atkins will pursue in his other poetry-dramas even as it remains largely within the purview of the law of genre.

Atkins' earliest published poetry-dramas, "The Drop of Blood" and "The Exoneration," along with a dramatic ballad, "Of Angela," appeared in his1961 book, *Phenomena*. As the book's title suggests, the dramatic poem and poetry-dramas are investigations into the phenomenology of rhetorical-narrative "objects" and their aesthetic "effects." To that end, Atkins deploys the affective sphere to destabilize the received genres of poetry and drama by underscoring rhetoric's power over narrative. At the rhetorical level this means projecting social roles over proper names. Thus "The Drop of Blood" is another critique of matrimony as it features an unnamed wife and unnamed husband. Its central "character," however, is a drop of blood that relentlessly mocks the wife's steadfast faith in the fidelity of her husband. Like the monomaniacal bird in "The Raven," or the insistent heartbeat beneath the floorboards in the "Tell-Tale Heart," the drop of blood—the wife's, of course—is a manifestation of the failure of repression. Indeed, we find out in the first scene that the wife cut her finger the day before while slicing cake. Our intimation that an anniversary or birthday has just passed—at any rate, some celebratory event—is reinforced by the wife's insistence, *pace* the drop of blood, that she is happy and in love. Still, she complains about a persistent headache and is "weary." As in so many of Poe's short stories and poems where physical debilitation is an index of psychological instability, so too the headache and drop of blood reflect the tension between the rhetoric of faith and the psychosomatics of repressed knowledge. This gap between rhetoric and the subconscious manifests itself on other levels, e.g., the distance between the wife's and husband's ages: "she is a woman aged 59" and he is "a young man in his early twenties." After the husband informs his wife that he will be "late" and departs, the drop of blood plays Iago to the wife's Othello, filling her head with suspicion regarding her husband's fidelity. Her worries are confirmed in Scene II which opens in an allegorical setting:

> *A metropolitan park. The Husband and a young woman enter. There is a Fountain of Inevitable Fate. Beside the Fountain is an apple tree wanting in height. On its bough sits a white Bird of Suspicion. Fountain and Bird are surrounded with the Leaves of Emotion. The Husband and The Young Woman are seen in pantomime as they embrace. (Phenomena, n.p.)*

Allegory, understood as a mode of "conspicuous technique," subordinates narrative to concept. Translated into a psychoanalytic model, allegory is the unveiling of the subconscious. The inconsistency of description (the phrase "the young woman" is not capitalized at the outset) and perspective (do the "Leaves of Emotion" belong to the "apple tree wanting height" or another tree?) is yet another sign of the wife's subconscious fears and emotional instability. The park "is" the drop of blood, an exterior "scene" of psychosomatic turmoil, one sign of which is the compulsion to repeat. Thus the white Bird of Suspicion here reappears, in a different form, in Scene III: "As in a summons to a word of thought I'd had,/ A suddenness of white appeared and fled./ Anxieties for a woman as happy as I am?" In brief, the scene is Grecian; the leaves speak as a "(verse choir)," the chorus of community, while the fountain's "(voice echoes as in cave)," recalls Plato's allegory of primitive unenlightenment. The adulterous couple, a kind of unrepentant Adam and Eve, "walk slowly deeper into the Park," deluded by the dream of a return to the atavistic pre-matrimonial. All the while the fountain recalls Keats' Grecian urn: "I'm the alas of a vessel that often holds/ Lovers briefly reflected in a marble mold." Like Poe's raven, the drop of blood mocks with repetition the wife's faith: "Expect me! / In the headache that so long severes/ Expect me!/ A footfalling persistence inside your ear!" The extravagant rhetoric—Atkins is fond of anastrophe, anthimeria, and zeugma—of "conspicuous technique" overwhelms the hackneyed plot in the same way that the music of opera can help one ignore librettos that strain credulity. When the wife kills her husband, herself and thus the drop of blood at the end of the poetry-drama, that violence is merely a repetition of the violence to the language Atkins accomplishes. Only in this Shakespearean slaughter do the rhetorical-aural and narrative dovetail, a defiant thrust at the norms of bourgeois life: money, marriage and property. This does not mean, however, that Atkins longs for a pre-capitalist aristocratic world. As the dramatic ballad "Of Angela" indicates, Atkins, like Baudelaire and Pound, can be equally critical of the corruptibility that infects a dying aristocracy.

"Of Angela" examines homosexuality as a tool of vengeance by a corrupt aristocracy against impotent working class heterosexuality. Once again a triangle is in play, this time between the aristocratic Laird and the unemployed working class member Joe, both of whom "belong" to the vain, pretentious Angela. Laird plays the piano, reads poetry and philosophy and is in love with Angela. She rebuffs his attentions, however, mocking Laird's insistence that "dreams give man his nobility." Her stinging rejoinders—"...Listen, what's/this 'Rilke' to me, or somethin' or other in Paris?/Just shit...//You're a bore! A goddamned bore!!!"—drive Laird to vengeance. After discovering that Joe, her fiancé, needs a loan (he never asks about a job), he makes a deal. He will give Joe the money if he engages in a homosexual relationship with Laird, not because Laird is attractive to Joe but because he wants to punish Angela. When Angela stumbles upon the lovers, she is disgusted and storms out of Laird's apartment. Joe runs after her to explain, a scream is heard, and Joe returns to inform Laird that Angela "fell" and killed herself. Laird wants Joe to stay with him and explain to the police but Joe's self-loathing, apparently riled after seeing himself through Angela's eyes, explodes as projection: he kills Laird and runs off from his "dead responsibilities." Although we might be tempted to imagine that if Atkins identified with any of these rather unsavory characters it would be the aesthete Laird who, like Atkins, loves poetry, philosophy and classical music, it is Joe who encapsulates Atkins' sense of himself as a man caught between unappetizing "choices." Joe has no interest in "work" and seems lukewarm about marrying. His willingness to engage in a homosexual relationship for money—which Atkins could only see as a form of debasement—points to Atkins' indignation that a man has to have, has to struggle for, money.[9] Of course, given Atkins' interest in Poe we might also understand Laird and Joe as two facets of the "same" person, the brute as the subconscious of the aesthete and, most important, both as social pariahs within a materialistic culture that apotheosizes "hard work." In short, this composite, hypothetical figure, perennially dissatisfied with the past and the present, would be Atkins' equivalent of Baudelaire's *flaneur*, the urban wanderer whose only solace is that one day, perhaps, his excoriations of a lost past and modernity will be set to music. As we will see below Atkins does, in fact, compose just such a figure even if he is, like so many of Poe's aristocratic figures (e.g., Usher), D.O.A.

The last piece in *Phenomena*, "The Exoneration," is the most unusual, perhaps the only, *play*—it is, apparently, not to be set to music—that Atkins published. Although it has some of the rhetorical features of his other poems and dramas (for example, as in "A Drop of Blood," the characters are named by their social roles), it is largely written in the rough brogue of policemen "interrogating" a prisoner through physical force. Comprised of one act, two scenes, this *bona fide* play embodies Poe: compression of structure and action. The entire play takes place in a police station; the two scenes are set in the interrogation room (Scene I) and the office where the desk cop and detective converse (Scene II). A man has been arrested for murder and the police are attempting to brutalize a confession out of him. However, he refuses to give them their drop of blood; his insistence on his innocence amounts to sealing himself within the vacuum of his conscience. After the "real" criminal is arrested the police report that the prisoner being interrogated has died. However, the prisoner staggers from the interrogation room, shocking the policemen, and is escorted out by the desk cop, who repeats the one refrain in the play: "We've Quaker'd jails:/ Franklin'd penalties:/ Emerson'd justice." The desk cop's insistence that humanism has triumphed over barbarism is, of course, belied by the violence—both corporeal and rhetorical—that comprises the bulk of the play.

Why does Atkins not subtitle this play "to be set to music"? Is it because it is not a poetry-drama? It has some of the rhetorical features of the works designated as poetry-dramas, for example, the apostrophe d that converts nouns into verbs, a favorite device of Atkins. Is there no music imaginable for law enforcement however corrupt?[10] Or is it simply that insofar as this work best represents Poe's insistence on compression and condensation no music is needed? After all, there is really no plot, no narrative, in "The Exoneration." In other words, there is very little for Atkins' rhetorical-aural devices to overwhelm or transcend. "The Exoneration" is nothing but rhetorical-aural violence; it plays off of, refers to, nothing. The tension between conspicuous technique as rhetorical-aural effects and melodramatic narratives and plots is missing here. When the detective is asked if the police should find out the name of another dead prisoner, the detective's response serves to close the play: "Fuck that!" Although the stock figures are never named, much less identified by ethnicity or race, it is not difficult to read this play about police brutality as one of Atkins' "black" dramas, not because only blacks are brutalized by policemen but because "black" has become the signifier of oppression, as Yoko Ono and John Lennon apparently recognized in their controversial recording "Woman Is The Nigger of the World."

Although it bears little formal or thematic similarity to Atkins' other dramatic efforts, the desk cop's belief in "progress," despite the evidence around him, is not that different from Laird's delusional infatuation with vanity in "Of Angela" or the wife's delusional love for her husband in "A Drop of Blood." And just as Joe survives his double humiliation before Angela and Laird, so too the prisoner, beaten nearly to death, walks out of the police station, with the help of the desk cop. Given Atkins' interest in the violence of effect, in "conspicuous technique," it is perhaps not surprising that, as in Poe, the violence of vice trumps the virtues. And insofar as these vices derive from institutions of social, moral and political authority—the family, work and law—it is also not surprising that in "The Seventh Circle," "a poem in radio format," published in his 1968 book *Heretofore*, Atkins' protagonist attempts to disavow every bourgeois allegiance. However, before we examine this singular "poem in radio format" I want to examine two more poetry-dramas that reinforce Atkins' sense that both vice and virtue belong, in large part, to a humanist bourgeois past from which the artist must be freed.

The consequences of humanist values, of remaining bound to the past, are explored in "The Abortionist" and "The Corpse," published in the 1963 book *Two By Atkins*. Taken together, these plays offer a rather moribund view of the economic, social and cultural possibilities within American life. Judging by the "non-American," and thus anachronistic, names assigned to the two primary male characters in the plays, Dr. Drassakar and Larenuf, the past is dead, and the future, uncertain. In "The Abortionist" Dr. Drassakar is a medical doctor whose career has been stymied by the father of his patient, Miss Harrington, who comes to him for an abortion, illegal at this time. Because of her father's interference in his career, Drassakar has been reduced to illegal back-alley procedures to make a living. Thus the title of the play refers to both doctors—Dr. Drassakar and Dr. Harrington—and their illegal "practices." Both procedures—one medical, one social—come down to the "same" thing—arresting the development of a potential human being, the "man" Drassakar could have been, the baby Miss Harrington might have had. Atkins' play rehearses a theme predominant in African American literature from Chesnutt to Ellison and beyond: the de-professionalization, due to persistent racism, of those professionally trained after Reconstruction (and perhaps after the Civil Rights Movement). Moreover, the Orientalism of Drassakar's name, suggesting an Egyptian heritage, if not actual ancestry, dramatizes what has been lost for naught: the glory that was Egypt's, to paraphrase Poe, has not been recompensed by economic, social or cultural "progress" in the United States of the 20th c. Finally, the differences between Drassakar and Miss Harrington are dramatized by their rhetoric. Whereas Harrington speaks in the normative, standard American English of the "present," Drassakar's rhetoric shuttles back and forth between "present" American and "past" British—that is, Elizabethan—speech, emphasizing that his over-acculturation may well be understood as an index of spatial (geographical) and temporal (historical) dislocation.

While "The Abortionist" portrays Drassakar as the trace of a past unable to embody itself in a present, "The Corpse" reverses the gender dynamics of one of Poe's favorite themes—a man mourning a dead woman who is yet "alive"—by depicting a widow unable to free herself from the memory of her dead husband, Larenuf. Specifically, she returns to his grave—over days, over weeks, and eventually, over the course of a year—until he meets what she calls his "second death." The Christian allusion is made explicit in Scene II of the opening act: "If we were the Awaited only and had come/ To salvage you out of death as out of tomb—/To take you home!" Having reversed the widower/dead woman paradigm of Poe, Atkins makes another remarkable revision: he asks us to imagine what might be possible "If we"—not Jesus—"were the Awaited only." Atkins does not complete the if/then logic of this conditional relationship; we are left with unfettered speculation regarding what the future might have been had it derived from a humanist past unadulterated by Christianity. Unlike the widow who has gazed upon the corpse of her deceased husband so often, so reverently, that she has aged prematurely, collapsing at the play's end , we, the play implies, are to turn toward tomorrow.[11] The difference, of course, would be that though both the secular and sacred futures are indeterminate (unless one subscribes to the Calvinist doctrine of predestination and election), the Christian is instructed to have "faith," to inscribe hope into history or, and it amounts to the same thing, ascribe hope to history. Is there "hope" in Atkins' drama? It all depends on how we read the name of the deceased. Larenuf is an anagram of *flaneur*, the urban wanderer normally associated with Baudelaire but also an aspect of the life of one of his major influences, Poe. Like Drassakar, the *flaneur* is dislocation incarnate, a man caught between the decline of one world and the advent of another. Unable to accept the corruption of the former and the decadence of the latter, he is a figure of ambivalence, of estrangement, and thus a kind of secular prophet insofar as he also encapsulates the uncanny. Perhaps no line in "The Corpse" sums up this sense of finding ourselves at a lost than this one: "Kissable he is. Yet he is from kissing far." The irreversibility of history, of lost, and thus of lack, is also, as Lacan reminds us, the structure of desire and thus, per Freud, of compulsion. We may thus understand the Widow's repeated trips to the grave as an enactment of the *fort/da* game, of acceptance and refusal, of affirmation and denial so central to the uncanny. She reenacts the back-and-forth of the *flaneur* in homage to the deceased who is a scrambled *flaneur*, perhaps an ex-*flaneu*r decomposing into the ruined remains of Larenuf. And to the extent we may "read" Larenuf as an insolvent *flaneur*, we may read the letters of his name as if they were tossed bones. In that sense we may understand Larenuf as Drassakar (the Widow notes "the setting/ Of his Sahara'd cheek...") by another name.

The narrator of what Atkins' subtitles "a poem in radio format," "The Seventh Circle," is another name for the one who stands apart, not omniscient, but disabused of many, if not all, humanist illusions. In Dante's *Inferno*, the seventh circle is reserved for the violent and so it seems appropriate that the narrator who, unlike Dante, must make his sojourn down into and out of hell alone, is the emblem of violence: he will attempt to destroy every bourgeois illusion. That he fails to do so is instructive; among other things, he has, by the very telling of this story, created art, and as noted above in the "Preface" art is merely one objectification of creativity in general. Yet it is not merely one among many other modes of creativity. Its privilcge as perhaps the ultimate form of human creation—and for Atkins it might be more important than the creation and birth of a human being—has long been waning. Almost all non-narrative modes of art—drama, poetry, sculpture, etc—have declined in direct proportion to the rise of the middle classes and the novel, the exception that proves the rule. In short, Atkins' decision to pursue three of the more rarified modes of art—avant-garde music, stylized drama, and experimental poetry—made him as inconsequential to the narrative of bourgeois life as the narrator of "The Seventh Circle." But why compose a "poem in radio format"? Atkins was writing during the heyday of radio dramatizations and he may well have understood that these were the formal and technological descendants of traditional theater. And just as most radio dramatizations were audio demonstrations of Poe's insistence on compression of action, a small number of characters and a plot driven toward the affective, so too "The Seventh Circle." Like the voiceover of a central figure, one usually morally compromised, in film noir—think *Sunset Boulevard* and *Double Indemnity*—radio dramas depended upon a narrator who was also a character in the program. So too "The Seventh Circle," perhaps a precursor to the poetry-dramas.[12] Its narrator sets up all four scenes but participates, as a character in dialogue with other characters, only in the last three. Yet, because he is present in all four scenes, we can imagine him as a silent, perhaps omniscient, observer in the opening scene, set in a "saloon." There, a bartender, man and woman comprise a microcosm of the "They" referred to in the narrator's opening monologue:

> There were many people who said that they
> were very much wrought up.
> They thought that something or other
> was inexpressibly bad.
> Although I was equally exposed to disturbances, I
> did not let them matter.
> If worse came directly at me, I did what was demanded
> in the face of fatalities.
> I did not allow myself than, perhaps,
> cruel feelings. (17)

Having set himself apart from "they," the narrator presents "Mosey's, a dense saloon that aired a thick/ so-much of smoke" as Plato's cave, the only glimmer of enlightenment "a one-eyed aloft'd lamp" which "made something of light on a bartender/whitening forth and back." The allusions to Cyclops and The Golden Day chapter of Ellison's *Invisible Man* fuse into allegory: Mosey's is moseying, the shuffling in submission of the blind herd, the "they." Both the man and woman arguing over whether to stay or leave (as the man says, "We got anything else to do? Go home—go to bed!/ Get up and get to work!") and the four plant workers who enter at the end of the scene constitute, for the narrator, the "collective panic" of "disturbances." Still, per his opening monologue, he "dared not let little things truly matter." Having dismissed the disturbances of labor, the narrator, in Scene II, calls on his "date," Lydia, yet another "one of the disturbances," at her apartment. He brings ginger ale; she has the spirits. Yet, as he looks on her with profound disinterest, he notes, somewhat ironically, that "Spirits that were once said to live in air/ would have been of some help." (19) In the postlapsarian world in which he finds himself, the narrator tries to tell Lydia that she should "possess" herself. She notes that he has always been "Too much" self-possessed. He disagrees: "Never enough, at least not as difficulties demand./ Now, I want to be immovable." (20) The allusion to young Stephen Daedalus' insistence on stasis as the highest achievement of art, on indifference as the proper posture of the artist (a god "paring his fingernails"), foreshadows the narrator's recognition in Scene IV that he has "not [been] at peace" insofar as he "had let the disturbances matter somehow." He has "allowed [himself] the cruel feelings,/ but cruel feelings were not trustworthy: they were the shadows of the containing/ self-accusatory." (26) The "shadows of the containing" take us back to Plato's cave, to Mosey's, for example, where "cruel feelings" are merely a reflection of impotence as the argument between the man and woman demonstrates. And though he has quit his job at J.J. McCauley in Scene III, refused to marry Lydia in Scene II, the narrator has not shed himself of the ramifications, the effects, of bourgeois ideology. He is still in the seventh circle, though he now knows that the way back "up," the way to a possible future, requires the armor of indifference and a rhetoric of refusals to be set to music.

Atkins never finished setting his poetry-dramas and dramatic poems to music. What remains of his work in drama points to a future of experimentation, one taken up by a number of avant-garde figures and movements. In elevating effect to the pinnacle of aesthetic achievement, Atkins affirmed his commitment to shattering the values of the bourgeoisie, not for political reasons, but in service to the freedom of the artist and, concurrently, the freedom of the reader.[13] In his most successful poetry-dramas—"The Abortionist," "A Drop of Blood," "The Corpse," "The Exoneration" and "The Seventh Circle"—Atkins demonstrated that the ideas of Poe and the New Critics still could serve as valuable resources for the artist who wished to push art to the limits of creativity.

Works Cited

Atkins, Russell. "Description of Poems-In-Play-Form (Word-Sets) As Poetry-Drama."*Juxtapositions*. Cleveland, Ohio: self-published, 1991.

____. "Egocentrical Projection As Object In EP Perspective." *Juxtapositions*. Cleveland, Ohio: self-published, 1991.

____. "Henry Dumas: An Appreciation," *Black American Literature Forum,* Vol. 22, No. 2, Henry Dumas Issue (Summer, 1988), pp. 159-160.

____. "Manifesto." *Juxtapositions*. Cleveland, Ohio: self-published, 1991.

____. "Of Angela." *Phenomena*. Wilberforce, Ohio: The Free Lance Poets and Prose Workshop/Wilberforce University Press, 1961.

____."Preface." *Juxtapositions*. Cleveland, Ohio: self-published, 1991.

___ ."Russell Atkins, 1926-." Farmington Hills, MI: Gale/Cengage Learning: Contemporary Authors Autobiography Series, 1995.

____. *The Abortionist. Two By Atkins*. Cleveland, Ohio: Free Lance Press, 1963.

____. *The Corpse. Two By Atkins*. Cleveland, Ohio: Free Lance Press, 1963.

____. *The Drop of Blood. Phenomena*. Wilberforce, Ohio: The Free Lance Poets and Prose Workshop/ Wilberforce University Press, 1961.

____. *The Exoneration. Phenomena*. Wilberforce, Ohio: The Free Lance Poets and Prose Workshop/ Wilberforce University Press, 1961.

____. "The Following Misconceptions Relating to My Poetry-Dramas, Poems-in-Play-Form, etc. (Subtitle: Somewhat silly comments made by others as 'critics'.)" *Juxtapositions*. Cleveland, Ohio: self-published, 1991.

_____. *The Nail.* Cleveland, Ohio: Free Lance Press, 1970.
_____. *The seventh circle. Heretofore*. London: Paul Breman (Heritage Series), 1968.
Ellison, Ralph. *Shadow and Act.* New York: Random House/ Vintage, 1964.
Poe, Edgar Allan. "A Philosophy of Composition." Philadelphia, PA: *Graham's American Monthly Magazine of Literature and Art*, 1846.

Notes

[1] See Atkins' essay "A Psycho-Visual Perspective For Musical 'Composition'" in which he emphasizes, as he does elsewhere, that his poetry and poetry-dramas are based less on literary sources (e.g., Shakespeare and Poe) than musical ones (in particular the sonata). Nonetheless, my argument is not that Atkins was "influenced" by these literary sources but rather that his ideas and values are consonant with those prevalent throughout the 19th and early 20th centuries.
[2] Both Tom Orange and Julie Patton have told me that they have heard some of this music on tape cassettes Atkins made. However, I have not been able to verify this information.
[3] By "violence" I refer to Atkins' interest in a Baroque -cum-Romantic musical tradition that emphasizes expressiveness over impression. Thus, in "Preface," he writes, " ...in the dramas, poetry is based on *orchestral* poetics...It is scored like a ton of bricks, using words for maximum momentum, volume, and *'doubling' by manipulating the implicit in a set of grammatical categories* as, e.g., a single melody upon two different sounding instruments*..." Among other things this explains Atkins' criticism of atonal music in general and serialism in particular
[4] As he writes in his brief note "Egocentrical Projection as Object in EP Perspective," which appears in *Juxtapositions*, "A technique should not serve meaning but rather meaning must not only *be* but SERVE technique." This asymmetrical relationship between the semantic and syntactical modes of an artwork, understood as an object that simply "is," is closer to the early or first generation of New Critics (and their 19th century predecessors) than the the more 'moderate' second generation represented by Blackmur et al.
[5] For example, the various fallacies that amount to reducing the artwork to the psychology or life of the artist, and

Pound's insistence that *who* writes great poems is irrelevant; it only matters that they be written.

[6] Not elsewhere, however. In the acerbic interview, "The Following Misconceptions Relating to My Poetry-Dramas, Poems-in-Play-Form, etc. (subtitle: Somewhat silly comments made by others as 'critics')," published in *Juxtapositions*, Atkins brushes aside the concerns of the audience in terms of the accessibility of art: "...a public which says in effect that it doesn't ask artists to write music, poetry, etc., and doesn't want them or need them and does not intend to pay for them, is, in my opinion, in no position to offer inane critical comment as to what 'works' given the subjective nature of that word. (p. 24)

[7] Ralph Ellison makes a similar point regarding presumptions about what is and isn't African American culture in his essay "The Little Man at Chehaw Station," published in *Shadow and Act.*

[8] The concept of a total work as embodying sundry genres is, of course, another way of saying that the books of Atkins are librettos for operas that hearken back to Greek and Roman antiquity when the distinctions between poetry, drama and music were less formulaic despite the attempts of Aristotle, Horace and others to codify generic distinctions.

[9] See Atkins' brief autobiographical essay in Gale's Contemporary Authors Autobiography Series where he discusses his frustration growing up in a culture where he was expected to work for money as he explored the various facets of his desire to be an artist of some kind.

[10] All the poetry-dramas concern Poe's favorite short story themes; the love of the living for the dead, romantic love gone awry and murder.

[11] A gesture not distant from Jesus' dictum to let the dead bury the dead except of course it is Jesus who is dead.

[12] Because it is impossible to ascertain when certain works were written, it may well be that both this "poem in radio

format" and "The Exoneration" represent different modes of creativity rather than indices of "artistic development."

[13] In his brief homage to Henry Dumas, published in, *Black American Literature*, Atkins opens the piece by qualifying his praise of the young author: "I find it quite possible to admire Dumas's work for its many virtues without caring for much of the subject matter. Sheer ability rescued him from a sort of disaster of digressions when his poetry and short stories took up such issues as lynching, African iconography, "Harlem," or Sixties-like sentiments, as in "Cuttin Down to Size." I have found myself wondering, momentarily, whether or not he chose to be too responsible and expended time on directions diverging somewhat from his real talent but in line with feelings that interfered. (When you feel strongly about injustices, it may be better sometimes not to allow them to distract the art-better to join a social service organization, do volunteer work, and let that suffice.)"

Atkins: Writing Cleveland

Sean Singer

Russell Atkins is a poet from Cleveland, and the urban environment is a vital source for his imagination. Urban life, and specifically black urban life, is important to his work. Cleveland, and the cultural imagination of Cleveland, are "main characters" in most of Atkins' work, and his ties to Cleveland also tie him to two of his poetic fathers, Hart Crane and Langston Hughes.[1]

Cleveland is a black majority city, and Atkins uses his poetic style—a "beyond category" approach to language—to illuminate the tensions between the aspirations Cleveland's blacks had for the so-called "American dream" even as Jim Crow's barriers to entry into that dream made obstacles to realizing them. Cleveland, with its frigid winds and low brick buildings, is divided into several neighborhood districts identified by whether they're east or west of the Cuyahoga River. Some districts, like Shaker Heights, had racially mixed populations and were middle-class.[2] A former industrial center, Cleveland also had many mixed-use areas suggesting something of its history in steel and manufacturing. Parts of Cleveland are violent, and this mayhem is bound with its Jim Crow past; for example, in addition to barring African Americans from hotels, businesses, and restaurants, for many years Cleveland had no parks near its black districts (Kusmer 58).

In a poem called "Waiting in Line at the Bank," Atkins describes the insidious practice known as "red-lining," wherein blacks were barred from getting loans to buy homes: "Qualified for the officer's glaring, / His unsteady mind on his revolver. / (That's responsibility's difference) / Brute hysteria quite likely." Later, the speaker becomes increasingly anonymous after a "circuitous break": "Systems analysts are working at it. / They needn't be as responsible / Nor as officious in the schema. / It's a natural enough probability: / That which gives money takes it away."

Here, the speaker is no longer an individual, but realizes "there's no stopping all this," and that "All's changed to a tenuousness / pitched against quasars."

Frequently there is an oblique tension in Atkins' urban poems in which private memory and public space align in surprising ways. Dolores Hayden offers a helpful insight about this:

> Identity is intimately tied to memory: both our personal memories (where we come from and where we have dwelt) and the collective or social memories interconnected with the histories of our families, neighbors, fellow workers, and ethnic communities (9).

Here, Hayden describes the ways memory is place-oriented, and contends that because the urban landscape evokes visual memory, it is an underutilized resource for public history(47).

During Atkins' productive years, Cleveland's black communities had varying configurations of property ownership and political participation. In "New Storefront," for example, the hopefulness for upward mobility remains fraught with tension:

Afresh'd with paint, the shop had glare:
chrome-plated the squared of for sale,
angles, or with glamorous rounds.
Auto Supply Co.
The owner looked too outright
(dart of a much refracted stare).
Aluminum had set him blind awhile—
the false going virtue of hope

no public interest anywhere about

The poem is only 15 lines long and words like *glare*, *chrome-plated, refracted, sheen, glimmered,* and *silver* resonate strongly, suggesting the way the shop's gleaming auto parts blind the owner to his own naivety. The speaker's pathos for a neighborhood "proliferous" with beauty parlors, barbeque joints, bars, and barbershops suggests how service industries dominate in the black community, while those based on production (e.g., Auto Supply Co.) face precarious circumstances.

The poem "Irritable Songs" makes this more explicit. In section 4, Atkins turns from irritability to anger, leaving behind, for the moment, disruptive syntax and figurative language:

shock the bastards:
eschew employment and the years
of such employment's benefits:
Social Security and Credit Unions
Retirement Funds, Insurances!
amidst recession, quit a job
and lack payments and credit cards!
here's another: go through
hospitals and have x-rays
or a complete checkup

then wait
for the collection agency!

This poem is so fresh and topical it could have been written this morning. Atkins suggests in poem after poem how, influenced by considerations of race, he is drawn to angularity and tension in the urban environment, seeking ways to create a subterfuge to escape that ambivalence, even if it means mining the caustic, often painful remains of the urban spaces that ignited his imagination in the first place. "Irritable Songs," like "New Storefront," makes a labor-side argument: we should have free health care, free education, and be paid a living wage.

Atkins also shows how the city's marginalized citizens, particularly the sick or elderly, deserve our particular attention. The patients in "Out of Patience at the Out-Patient Clinic," for example, clamor with bedpans and soiled dishes, while the staff, "from debt, aloof," buy "a farm near Oregon / or go ... to the Bahamas for the summer." Similarly, in "While Waiting for Friend to Come to Visit a Friend in a Mental Hospital," Atkins writs, "the attendant has ideas about me // the attendant keeps watch, watching / that abrupt wild uranium grow a bat's ears, / sardine flowers, moons' eggs, / stomach guitars." The poem remains ambiguous (and ambivalent) about whether the speaker is the friend in the hospital or the friend waiting to visit the friend.

Cleveland's landscape is central to Atkins' work; he does not do portraiture, but often describes it via a removed speaker who is embodied by the passionate syntax in the poem. Like Hart Crane, who said he was interested in "the so-called illogical impingements of the connotations of words on the consciousness (and their combinations and interplay in metaphor on this basis)," Atkins, too, is fascinated by perceptions. His poems, thus, are both expressionistic and impressionistic.

In "On the Fine Arts Garden, Cleveland," Atkins imagines:

all things
softly
and pouring with
mellows the silver fountain
silent figures
move reposefully into the living shadows
and then the golden lamps
the while

slowly filtering—

The poem's feeling is created by its fairly traditional imagery (silver and gold, lamps and shadows) and the metaphor's referent has more to do with creating an emotion anew than recalling an emotion. The relationship between the concept of the poem and the sound-images used to transmit the dynamics of metaphor is psychological.

Both Atkins and Crane were raised in somewhat coddled circumstances, primarily by their mothers. Yet, where Crane was expected to join his father's candy manufacturing business, Atkins was raised in an environment of artistic refinement (Caruso, piano lessons, Latin, painting, etc.) and was expected to become an artist. His family was anti-jazz and anti-blues, which they considered "bad, naughty" (Atkins 3). This affectation was common among black bourgeoisie in the 1920s.[3] The irony of his Gramma's, Aunt Mae's, and Mama's religiosity is hinted at in "Old Man Carrying a Bible in a High Crime Area": "Condense, will it? grow a barrel / for shooting?" The poem ends with a comic punchline: "Old friend, listen: don't wait / — when they come at you, / throw it at them!"

Around 1928, when he was two, Russell Atkins was hidden in a dilapidated room by his Gramma who sought to protect him from a "hant," or haunt, who darkened his complexion and wanted to make their lives miserable.

(These hants have a long history in Afro-American musical lore, particularly the blues, and are related to "goofer dust," "hoodoo," "jinxes," "mojo," "juju," "gris-gris," and "zu-vembies.") Gramma Atkins would murmur to her hant all day, and believed Russell's phenotype to be caused not by genetics, but by their devious machinations. Atkins' early recollections of this hant are related to his uniqueness, his "beyond category" status as a writer insofar as they allow him to write without fear of ghosts, the memories of parents and authority figures (Atkins 2).

Atkins, an original among black American writers of his generation, remains far outside the canon today, though he has achieved a kind of cult status among cognoscenti[4]. One of the defining characteristic of his poems is a kind of bravery: Atkins writes without fear of voices of authority figures, teachers, and parents—ghosts in a writer's head who tell him him, "don't think that," or "don't try that." Literal and metaphorical ghosts and specters abound in his work:

> what afars for me? nears,
> contortioning its ectoplasm?
>
> ("Spectres, Spectres")

> I thought, had failed at night,
> and the insidious, spectral
> would wear away with someone's funeral
>
> ("Prelude: Dawn")

> a wraith waving a grey scarf
>
> ("Irritable Songs")

These entities suggest the empty spaces between Atkins' private memory of childhood and the public history of Cleveland with which he is often concerned.

Atkins was dedicated to all things avant-garde, and his

magazine, *Free Lance* (launched in 1950) reflects that. He has consistently written outside the boundaries of traditional poetic style, his poems often not meant to communicate so much as exist as objects built from language. He is interested primarily in aesthetics: intervallic leaps and highly figurative language that exaggerates and disarranges grammar.

His figurative language is often as fresh now as it was when it was written, pushing against the pressure of the line and creating moments of ecstatic beauty:

Measure his blood pressure then by
the wildest tendrils
both overgrown
both by the cruel'd edges
("For a Neighbor Stricken Suddenly")

the heap twists up
hardening the unhard, unhardening
the hardened
("It's Here In The")

Thunder crammed in a moan.

Craze of the seascape!
("Lake in a Storm")

Oh didn't it " " "   " " " " " "
" "   " "
" "   " "
" "   " "
"
" "   "
" "
" "
" "   " "

rain
("Spyrytual")

I drew to her while she
                                        into the air
smiled x
            THUNDER
                                        ("A fantaisie")

As these few examples illustrate, many of the tropes common to his work—repetition, rhetorical transversal, a comic voice amid the gloom, and the use of white space as a mode of interrogation—show themselves frequently in his work. Except for the lovely concrete poem, "Spyrytual"—which employs quotation marks for raindrops and alludes to the pop spiritual sung with enthusiasm by the world's greatest gospel singer, Mahalia Jackson, at the Newport Jazz Festival in 1958—Atkins' work does what poems ought to do: it metes out truth and beauty in inventive, energetic ways.

Atkins' most inimitable sonic characteristic (though it has a long history of precedents in English poetry) is his use of the apostrophe-d (*'d*), which appears all the time in his work: *weary'd, skull'd, antenn'd, up'd, thrall'd, quick'd, stark'd, vicious'd, torso'd, slab'd*, etc. He appends the *'d* to both verbs and nouns, instantly freshening or sharpening the syntax. Atkins says he "resuscitated it, so to speak, to specify a bold distortion of the weak verb which I use to exaggerate and disarrange the grammar" ("The Following Misconceptions..." 15). Oddly, its effect is both formal, because it suggests a link to Chaucer, Whitman, and others, and informal, because of its relationship to spoken language on the street: the clipped ends of words, quickly said.

The third most interesting quality of Atkins' work is related to his use of the *'d*, what he calls "intervallic substitutions…the avoidance of the strictly diatonic in harmonic modulation in avant-garde (or contemporary) 'musical' composition" ("Tbe Following Misconceptions..." 16). (In terms of jazz, Atkins' contemporary Eric Dolphy is known to have used intervallic substitutions as a defining characteristic.[5]) It is interesting to note that "interval" literally means "the space between ramparts," and its common abstract meaning, "interval of space or time," is derived from its concrete meaning. These intervals in Atkins' poems reduce their function in terms of sense, but often heighten their imaginative leaps, metaphoric capability, and move their speakers' psychic distance from wide-apart to close-up.

In some ways Atkins' aesthetic is an embrace of the African-American human being and a rejection of both cultural nationalism and cultural antebellumism, a mindset that expects people to stay in their places. In terms of poetry, Atkins adds possibilities instead of cutting them off. It may seem strange that Atkins, the quintessential outcast, was championed by the most iconic of black American writers, Langston Hughes.[6] Whereas Hughes often relied on blues form, archetypal tropes of doomed hetero-normative romance (despite his own homosexuality or asexuality), and simplicity of feeling, Atkins always goes for the edge of form, themes, and complexity. He is like late-period Coltrane to Hughes's early Coltrane.

Like Hughes, Atkins the poet inhabits the urban community. He walks its avenues and observes people, almost like a camera lens. In "Late Bus," for instance, Atkins tries to disrupt the relationship in the cultural imagination between the black male body and an entrenched idea of what it represents:

> Theft's hour—the bus
> against the hark lights
> afright from houses!
> Two dark men board laughing
> (their teeth, crooked)
> and take a seat in back,

two men in jeans, jackets:

the streets are deserted:
the bus blunders on, bounced!
—we wait:

the men sit still:
One talks to the other
yeah,—their eyes (—sure,
we know what's up—)
one feigns awhiled of sleep,
one coughs quickly as a signal
while the other holds—
now!
—watch their pockets,
their hands are moving:
one as for a cigarette
and one as if finding
matches
he reaches, reaches up
falsely to pull the bell
cord East 55
they leave the bus

it makes no difference:
four dark men board
—laughing

This poem elucidates most of the themes that thread themselves through Atkins' work. It's set in the urban environment, among the black community (note the plural first-person pronoun in line 10), and shows the men not as transparently violent symbols ("we know what's up") but as apparitions who represent social and communal fears among black people. They become the defense for others' desire. Atkins addresses a dilemma for black males that resonates with something William Pope.L has said: being male connotes privilege, but being black connotes a certain subordination and lack.[7] The figures on the bus seem to embody this tension to resolve the dilemma. Ideology is tied to their masculinity. The poem ends without punctuation as the men board laughing. Atkins deliberately makes it unclear who is speaking, or from where, but the poem leaves behind a sensation of calm desperation.

As we exit the bus, it becomes clear that urban life, specifically in Cleveland, is vital to understanding Russell Atkins' work. Since the 1940s, Atkins has pursued inventive ways of writing about his city and, in the process, created a "way-out" persona unlike any other. Like his poetic fathers from Cleveland, Hart Crane and Langston Hughes, he uses jazz-like intervals and leaps, loves urban locations and perspectives, makes use of passionately figurative and quirky language—and creates in the process poems that are both expressionistic and impressionistic. Atkins' voice is completely unique in American poetry and it can be challenging for most readers. To paraphrase the poet, through much music pours a supra light, as if it were preternatural grief. There is urban pathos in these poems, connecting private and public memory in fresh, fantastic ways.

Works Cited

Atkins, Russell. "Autobiography." *Contemporary Authors Autobiography Series.* Vol. 16. Detroit, MI: Gale Research Co., 1984.

—. "The Following Misconceptions Relating to My Poetry-Dramas, Poems-in-Play-Form, etc." *Juxtapositions.* Self-published, 1991.

Bessire, Mark H. E. *William Pope L.: The Friendliest Black Artist in America.* Cambridge, MA: MIT Press, 2002.

Hayden, Dolores. *The Power of Place: Urban Landscapes as Public History.* Cambridge, MA: MIT Press, 1997.

Kusmer, Kenneth L. *A Ghetto Takes Shape: Black Cleveland, 1870-1939.* Champaign, IL: University of Illinois Press, 1978.

Notes

[1] Crane was born and raised in Cleveland, and Hughes, though itinerate, attended high school in Cleveland in the 1910s.

[2] For example, the Cleveland-born avant-garde jazz saxophonist Albert Ayler had been a golf caddie at Cleveland's all-white courses and was captain of his school golf team.

[3] Jazz's bad reputation was connected to its being played in brothels in New Orleans, and possibly also because its musicians were trained in an oral environment rather than in conservatories.

[4] People are born every day, but by "generation," I include: James A. Emanuel (b. 1921), Mari Evans (b. 1923), Bob Kaufman (b. 1925), Ted Joans (b. 1928), and Etheridge Knight (b. 1931).

[5] Dolphy (1928-1964) played alto saxophone, flute, and bass clarinet. His wide intervals gives his music a distinctive sound, the way Atkins' intervals give his their distinctive sound.

[6] Atkins met Hughes through the Phillis Wheatley Association, a black social agency in Cleveland, in or around 1942, when Hughes was about 40 and Atkins was about 16.

[7] See also the Interview with William Pope L. by Lowery Stokes Sims in *William Pope L. The Friendliest Black Artist in America.* Cambridge: MIT Press, 2002, 62-63.

The Place of Atkins and Future Scholarship

Tom Orange

Dateline: Cleveland, Ohio. The headline in the December 12, 2012 *Plain Dealer* reads: "Green City Growers to plant first winter crop in large Cleveland greenhouse." One of three employee-owned, for-profit companies under the Evergreen Cooperatives umbrella (the other two are Evergreen Laundry Cooperative and Evergreen Energy Solutions), Green City Growers boasts a $17 million, 3.25-acre hydroponic greenhouse (one of the largest in the country) and expects to grow three million heads of salad greens and three hundred thousand pounds of herbs annually. Located between East 55th Street and Kinsman Road, in the long-blighted Central neighborhood, GCG offers a living wage and health insurance to nearly 40 employees and plans to market its produce to local grocers, hospitals, universities, and food service companies within a 150-mile radius.[1]

Not only has the project garnered international attention with coverage in *The Economist*, *The Nation* and *Business Week*, but its progress has been swift and impressive: awarded a $400,000 grant from The Cleveland Foundation in December 2010, GCG broke ground on the greenhouse itself in mid-October 2011; by early April, the day before I received page proofs for this essay, I purchased a delicious head of GCG lettuce at my local grocer for the first time.[2] Here is a clear success story in the fight against corporate agriculture, which is wasting exorbitant amounts of taxpayer dollars (through government subsidies) and fossil fuels (through transporting produce around the world) in order to sell us, in Michael Pollan's coinage, "edible food-like substances" that are literally making us sick if not killing us outright.[3]

In the history of green urban renewal in Cleveland, however, another date needs to be pointed out: October 1, 2010. Cleveland property tax records indicate that on this date, Burten, Bell Carr Development Inc. became owner of record for 6005 Grand Avenue, having purchased the property there from one "Phillip Atkins Russell" [sic].[4] Progress never comes without some costs: in this case the displacement of a reclusive, long-neglected octogenarian American poet from the place he called home for over fifty years.

—

This is not the first time progress has come with a cost to the residents of Grand Avenue. In the late 1920s, Grand Avenue was was bisected by the Nickel Plate Road, as the New York, Chicago & St. Louis Railroad had come to be known. Owned then by New York Central, the Nickel Plate was found by the Interstate Commerce Commission to be in violation of the 1914 Clayton Anti-Trust Act. It was sold in 1916 to Cleveland's infamous Van Sweringen brothers, enabling them to build their commuter rail from the wealthy suburb of Shaker Heights to their Union Terminal Tower downtown, a train station housed in, at the time of its completion in 1927, the tallest building in the world outside New York City, and the center of the Van Sweringens' commercial empire.[5]

Photographs taken in 1922 and 1926 by the NKP along

its right-of-way and adjacent neighborhoods show Grand Avenue then to be a fairly typical Cleveland thoroughfare, with its mixture of light and heavy industrial buildings and middle class homes.[6] Even by this time, however, demographic shifts that would eventually characterize much of the urban American landscape were well underway.

As it bisected Grand Avenue then, the Nickel Plate (now owned and operated by Norfolk Southern) today divides two east-side Cleveland neighborhoods: Central and Kinsman, named after major streets running through them. (With a few exceptions, Cleveland is not a city with well-defined neighborhoods; most local knowledge and self-identification comes from street intersections and blocks rather than neighborhoods). Central was initially populated during the 1830s by Germans, joined in the coming decades by Hungarians, Greeks, Italians and Jews. By the turn of the 20th Century, Central hosted a variety of retail businesses and factories while remaining relatively lower-middle class in its demographic: like many inner city neighborhoods, it was a place you would leave if you could. With the beginning of World War I, factory managers loosened racial restrictions and began hiring African Americans seeking better lives by the tens of thousands via The Great Migration from the South. Cleveland's African American population quadrupled between 1910 and 1920, with many of them moving to Central.[7] Another soon-to-be literati and one of Atkins' key early supporters, Langston Hughes, lived on East 86th Street between Cedar and Quincy (2 miles from where Atkins would live) and attended Central High School, writing in *The Big Sea* (1940):

> Central was the high school of students of foreign-born parents—until the Negros came. It is an old high school with many famous graduates. It used to be long ago the high school of the aristocrats, until the aristocrats

> moved farther out. Then poor whites and foreign-born took over the district. Then during the war, the Negros came. Now Central is almost entirely a Negro school in the heart of Cleveland's vast Negro quarter.

During the post-WWII economic boom experienced by much of the United States, Central followed most of Cleveland's inner city in seeing its population plummet: after its peak population of just under 70,000 in 1950, Central lost nearly 80% of its residents in fifty years, with a mere 12,000 residents by 2000. What little traffic Grand Avenue experienced when I began visiting Atkins at his home in Fall 2009 took place mostly on foot: scrappers pushing shopping carts to and from the metal recycling plant across the street from his house, the former site of the Ohio Confection Company (another reminder of our slave past, as Western sweet-tooths would not have been possible without the slave labor that was essential to the sugar industry).

And yet, to turn past today's cellphone and beauty supply stores of East 55th Street to Grand Avenue and neighboring side streets, one marvels not so much at the urban blight but at the urban pastoral left in its wake. Nature reclaims the work of humankind in mere decades. Less than a mile from Atkins' former home, where Grand Avenue picks up again on the other side of the Norfolk Southern tracks, just one block south on Rawlings Avenue, one can find the site of another great Cleveland artist's boyhood home: across the street from the former Rawlings Junior High School, the whole block is grown over in pasture, dotted with two or three houses at most, perhaps a few occupied. Here, a young Albert Ayler practiced his saxophone daily, on his way to changing jazz history.

To say Cleveland ignores, even willfully forgets, its innovative artists might be an understatement. A small plot of land at a bend in the Cuyahoga River astride the Columbus Avenue Bridge, hosting a huge metal sculpture by local artist Gene Kangas bearing words from Hart Crane's "The Bridge," otherwise bears no signage or any other indication that Crane grew up here; "Hart Crane Park" is a colloquial, not official designation. The burnt-out East Cleveland apartment building where d.a. levy, according to some interpretations of the still uncertain events, shot himself due in part to extended harassment and trumped-up pornography charges by the Cleveland police, bears no civic marker. No memorial exists to Albert Ayler, who was found dead in New York's East River under mysterious circumstances at the age of 34.

—

In a city with a history of suiciding its innovative artists, we might understand Russell Atkins' seclusion as the kinder, gentler alternative of a willful social death. He routinely remarked to me how much letters, phone calls and personal visits surprised him, since he figured most of the literary world had presumed him dead. My initial visits to Atkins at his home were motivated by the counter-ephemerality that has driven much of my poetry scholarship: having returned to my home town the previous year and only then begun studying up on Cleveland's perhaps most notorious forgotten poet, I wanted to assess Atkins' willingness to have some of his poetic dramas from the 1950s included in a forthcoming anthology of poets' theater pieces being edited by Patrick Durgin and Kevin Killian. Self-effacing to a fault, Atkins insisted no one would really be interested in those pieces today, but I insisted to the contrary. With each visit he grew more willing to share bits and pieces of his extensive literary archives with me: with some effort he could nearly always remember where in his cluttered but reasonably clean premises some relevant piece of ephemera resided: a xerox of a letter from Hughes, the glowing European reviews of his "Psychovisual Perspective for 'Musical' Composition" (1958). I never ventured, nor was I invited, beyond his living room, which only hinted at the sheer amount of additional literary matter he had collected over the decades and was storing upstairs.

The unfortunate reality of Atkins' displacement from Grand Avenue is that future scholarship will never fully know what archival materials (his own and those of the many poets Atkins knew and corresponded with over the years) were lost in the process. I am told by a close Atkins associate that 10 boxes of material survived the move; this is the only additional starting point for any archival work on Atkins (beyond the five boxes at the Woodruff Library in the Atlanta University Center and the Heritage Press materials donated by Paul Breman to the Vivian Harsh Collection of the Chicago Public Library). The directions for future Atkins scholarship I outline here are based on my understanding of Atkins materials at the time of my visits to him and may, in perhaps many cases, be rendered moot by his displacement from Grand Avenue.

Collected Writings - The present Unsung Masters edition serves several much-needed functions: first, as a stop-gap measure to prevent Atkins' work from drifting into complete obscurity; second, to raise awareness of his work and hopefully generate further readerly and scholarly interest in it. Beyond this, a "collected writings" strikes me as not only necessary but relatively simple to compile. Craig Dworkin's Eclipse project online hosts all of Atkins' book and chapbook publications online in both page-scan images and PDF files. Copying and pasting these files into an MS Word document, I was able to establish a working draft of Atkins' publications (poetry, prose, and poetic dramas) in chronological order in a matter of a few hours. In addition, a collected writings would, in my opinion, have to include his essay in music theory ("Psychovisual Perspective for 'Musical' Composition"), which has never been reprinted in any form since its initial appearance in the *Free Lance*. Not only was Atkins particularly proud of this work and the praise it earned from many European composers and theorists, but with the chief exception of Aldon Nielsen, literary critics and poets have almost universally ignored it. Atkins also routinely contributed reviews and short essays to the *Free Lance*, some of which may merit inclusion in a collected writings. Finally, the autobiography Atkins wrote on a commission from Gale's Contemporary Authors Autobiography Series (volume 16, 1992) is essential reading for any study of Atkins.

Complete Poems - Given that Atkins was perhaps his own harshest critic, the existence not only of multiple variant drafts of published poems but also of unpublished poems and drafts was likely quite high. Evidence from recordings of public readings he gave in 1963 and 1966, maintained by Joanne Cornelius at Cleveland State University, indicate that even then Atkins was reading poems that never appeared in any of his book or chapbook publications. But given also the archival materials that were lost in Atkins' displacement from Grand Avenue, any efforts to establish a "complete" text of his writing are likely doomed to failure. Uncollected poems published in periodicals since 1976 (his last book publication before this one) could certainly be compiled and included in a "collected" writings.

Poetry and Performance - Atkins recordings are conspicuously absent from Pennsound, Ubu.com and other hosts of avant-garde audio materials. The recordings at Cleveland State mentioned above both merit attention from performance scholars: the earlier recording is of poorer quality than the later, but again, both contain poems not available elsewhere and give ample demonstration of Atkins' approach to performance: dramatic, perhaps to a fault, but with frequently amusing and typically self-effacing between-poem commentary. On one of my visits to Grand Avenue, Atkins played me part of an audio cassette recording he made of himself reading one of his poetic-dramas (perhaps *The Abortionist*, I cannot recall). He thought I would find it too weird, but I insisted he play it: the recording showed that he performed all parts himself, male and female, in different voices. Again, whether this tape survived remains to be seen but surely could prove fruitful for further work on Atkins and performance studies, gender studies, etc.

Music - Perhaps the area of his creative activity even more neglected than his poetry, music was at least as important to Atkins as his poetry. When asked if he could list his musical compositions, he mentioned a cello sonata (from the 1970s), a violin sonata (date uncertain), a piano concerto (1987), several string quartets (dates uncertain), and collections of pieces for solo piano: *Objects* (1967) and *Spyrytuals* (twenty pieces clearly bearing some relation to the 1966 chapbook of the same name). Most of these pieces existed only in manuscript, notated on staff paper in Atkins' own hand, and hence would need to be transcribed and typeset by a trained musician or scholar before publication, let alone performance, could be possible. Atkins did have and played for me cassette recordings of some of these pieces, as performed in the 1970s by Hale Smith and other of his Cleveland music colleagues. Again, whether these recordings survived remains to be seen.

——

As we continue our headlong journey into the digital age and its attendant exponential proliferation of poetry and poetic forms, we can count our blessings that the Eclipse project and other websites are helping to preserve our poetic legacy while we curse how much of that same legacy our neglect is consigning to history's dustbin. Atkins' notorious reclusiveness surely debilitated his own legacy-building efforts, and yet I know I was not the first or last poet to visit Atkins at Grand Avenue and feel the sheer enormity of archival work that needed to be done there: one could feel its potential to consume one's entire life. And yet as poets and scholars, should we simply ape neoliberal *homo economicus*, with his self-serving individualism, his rampant consumerism, his growth at all costs, his self- and earth-suffocation in our own waste? Conservation, preservation and maintenance have to become equal partners with originality, innovation and progress if our poetical economies are going to become healthy.

6005 and 6009 Grand Avenue, Cleveland, OH

Notes

[1] Debbi Snook, "Green City Growers to plant first winter crop in large Cleveland greenhouse." *Plain Dealer*, 12 December, online at http://www.cleveland.com/taste/index.ssf /2012/12/green_ city_growers_to_plant_fi.html. See also "Green City Growers Greenhouse," http:// www.bbcdevelopment.org /development/ social-enterprise/hydroponi-greenhouse/.

[2] "Restoring Cleveland: Micro-projects aim to restore a shattered area," *The Economist*, 7 January 2010, online at http://www.economist.com/node/15213793?story_id=15 213793; Gar Alperovitz, "The Cleveland Model," *The Nation*, 1 March 2010, online at http://www.thenation.com/article/cleveland-model; John Tozzi, "Buying Local on a Large Scale," *Business Week*, 12 February 2010, online at http://www.businessweek.com/smallbiz/ content/feb2010/sb20100212_832582.htm.

[3] Michael Pollan, *In Defense of Food: An Eater's Manifesto* (New York: Penguin, 2008), page 1.

[4] City of Cleveland, "City Planning Commission GIS," online at http://planning.city.cleveland.oh.us/gis/cpc/ basemap.jsp. Built in 1915, 6005 Grand Avenue was a five-room, 1352 square-foot two story house with, before its demolition, an assessed value of $2400.00.

[5] Case Western Reserve University, "Encyclopedia of Cleveland History: Nickel Plate Road," online at http://ech. cwru .edu/ech-cgi/article.pl?id=NPR; "Encyclopedia of Cleveland History: Cleveland Union Terminal," online at http://

ech.cwru.edu/ech-cgi/article.pl?id=CUT.

[6] Cleveland State University, "The Cleveland Memory Project," http://www.clevelandmemory.org. (Search for "Nickel AND Grand")

[7] Case Western Reserve University, "Encyclopedia of Cleveland History: Central (Neighborhood)," online at http://ech.cwru.edu/ech-cgi/article.pl?id=CN5; City of Cleveland, "Cleveland Neighborhood Fact Sheets," online at http://planning.city.cleveland.oh.us/census/factsheets/spa19.pdf.

[8] Langston Hughes, "The Big Sea: An Autobiography" (New York: Macmillan, 1993), pages 29-30.

[9] "Eclipse," Craig Dworkin, ed., online at eclipsearchive.org.

Books by Russell Atkins

A Podium Presentation. Brooklyn Heights, OH: The Poetry Seminar Press, 1960. Poetry.

Objects. Eureka, CA: Hearse Chapbooks, 1961. Poetry.

Phenomena. Cleveland: The Free Lance Poets & Prose Workshop, 1961. Poetry. "A Poem-Play in Music Form to be set to music."

Objects 2. Cleveland: The Renegade Press, 1963. Poetry.

Two by Atkins: The Abortionist and The Corpse. Cleveland: Free Lance Poets and Prose Workshop, 1963. "Poetic dramas to be set to music."

Heretofore. London: The Heritage Series, edited by Paul Bremen, 1968. Poetry. "A poem in radio format."

The Nail. Cleveland & Atlanta: Free Lance Press, 1970. Verse-drama.

Maleficium. Cleveland & Atlanta: Free Lance Press, 1971. Prose.

Here in The. Cleveland: Cleveland State University Press, 1976. Poetry.

Whichever. Cleveland: Free Lance Press, 1978. Poetry.

Juxtapositions. Self-published, 1991. Poetry, essays, a manifesto.

Notes on the Contributors to this Volume

Aldon Lynn Nielsen is the George and Barbara Kelly Professor of American Literature at the Pennsylvania State University. His books of criticism include *Reading Race, Writing between the Lines, C.L.R. James: A Critical Introduction, Black Chant* and *Integral Music: Languages of African American Innovation.* His collections of poetry include *Heat Strings, Evacuation Routes, Stepping Razor, VEXT, Mixage, Mantic Semantic* and *A Brand New Beggar.*

Tom Orange teaches writing at Case Western Reserve University in Cleveland, Ohio. He curates art and poetry events at Brandt Gallery, SPACES Gallery and MOCA Cleveland; hosts "The Brewing Luminous," a weekly freeform radio program on WCSB 89.3 FM; and performs widely in the Cleveland rock and experimental music scenes.

To see more of cover photographer and painter **Charles J. Pinkney**'s work, go to www.charlespinkney.com.

Evie Shockley is the author of *Renegade Poetics: Black Aesthetics and Formal Innovation in African American Poetry,* as well as two books of poetry: *a half-red sea* and *the new black*, which won the 2012 Hurston/Wright Legacy Award in Poetry. She is Associate Professor of English at Rutgers University-New Brunswick.

Sean Singer's first book *Discography* won the Yale Series of Younger Poets Prize. He wrote his dissertation, "The Brick: Newark's Artistic Inquiry into Urban Crisis" in American Studies at Rutgers-Newark. He lives in New York City.

Tyrone Williams teaches literature and theory at Xavier University in Cincinnati, Ohio. He is the author of five books of poetry, *c.c.*, *On Spec*, *The Hero Project of the Century*, *Adventures of Pi,* and *Howell.* His website is at http://home.earthlink.net/~suspend

The Editors of This Volume

Kevin Prufer is the author of several books of poems, including *Fallen from a Chariot, National Anthem, In a Beautiful Country,* and *Churches.* He's also co-edited *New European Poets, Dark Horses: Essays on Overlooked Poems*, and, for the Unsung Masters Series, *Dunstan Thompson: on the Life & Work of a Lost American Master.* He is a professor in the Creative Writing Program at the University of Houston.

Michael Dumanis is the author of the poetry collection *My Soviet Union*, winner of the Juniper Prize for Poetry, and coeditor of the anthology *Legitimate Dangers: American Poets of the New Century.* Formerly the Director of the Cleveland State University Poetry Center, he is a professor at Bennington College.

The Unsung Masters Series

...bringing into print books on great, underappreciated, and out-of-print authors. Titles include:

Laura Jensen: A Symposium. (As part of *Pleiades* magazine.) 2009. Edited by Kevin Prufer & Wayne Miller.

Dunstan Thompson: On the Life & Work of a Lost American Master. 2010. Edited by D.A. Powell & Kevin Prufer.

Tamura Ryuichi: On the Life & Work of a 20th Century Master. 2011. Edited by Takako Lento & Wayne Miller.

Nancy Hale: On the Life & Work of a Lost American Master. 2012. Edited by Dan Chaon, Norah H. Lind, & Phong Nguyen.

Russell Atkins: On the Life & Work of an American Master. 2013. Edited by Kevin Prufer & Michael Dumanis.